A Year
in Nature

First published in Great Britain in 2026 by Gaia, an imprint of
Octopus Publishing Group Ltd
Carmelite House
50 Victoria Embankment
London EC4Y 0DZ
www.octopusbooks.co.uk

An Hachette UK Company
www.hachette.co.uk

The authorized representative in the EEA is Hachette Ireland, 8 Castlecourt Centre, Dublin 15, D15 XTP3, Ireland (email: info@hbgi.ie)

This material was previously published in *The Almanac: A Seasonal Guide to 2019*, *The Almanac: A Seasonal Guide to 2020*, *The Almanac: A Seasonal Guide to 2021*, *The Almanac: A Seasonal Guide to 2022*, *The Almanac: A Seasonal Guide to 2023* and *The Almanac: A Seasonal Guide to 2024*

Text copyright © Lia Leendertz 2018, 2019, 2020, 2021, 2022, 2023, 2026
Design and layout copyright © Octopus Publishing Group Ltd 2026
Illustrations copyright © Celia Hart 2018, 2026; Julia McKenzie 2019, 2026; Helen Cann 2020, 2026; Harry Brockway 2021, 2026; Whooli Chen 2022, 2026 and Aitch 2023, 2026
Music copyright © Richard Barnard 2023, 2024, 2026

All rights reserved. No part of this work may be reproduced or utilised in any form or by any means, electronic or mechanical, including photocopying, recording or by any information storage and retrieval system, without the prior written permission of the publisher.

Lia Leendertz has asserted her right under the Copyright, Designs and Patents Act 1988 to be identified as the author of this work.

ISBN 978-1-8567-5599-3

A CIP catalogue record for this book is available from the British Library.
Printed and bound in the United Kingdom.

10 9 8 7 6 5 4 3 2 1

Publisher: Lucy Pessell
Senior Designer: Alicia House
Senior Editor: Katie Button
Assistant Editor: Samina Rahman
Production Controller: Sarah Parry
Cover illustration: Lucy Robertson

This FSC® label means that materials used for the product have been responsibly sourced.

Publisher's note:
Every effort has been made to establish copyright ownership of material included in this publication and the publisher apologises for any errors or omissions made.

A Year in Nature

A celebration of the seasons

From the bestselling author of
THE **ALMANAC**

LIA LEENDERTZ

Contents

Introduction	5
January	6
February	14
March	24
April	40
May	50
June	64
July	76
August	84
September	100
October	114
November	128
December	144

A Year in Nature

The natural world is all around you, scuttling along the hedgerow that lines your drive to work, fluttering through the trees you stroll beneath, in the soil of the allotment and the water of the canal. We have become good at insulating ourselves from it - a little too good, perhaps - and it is easy to feel that the natural world lies elsewhere, on our seaside holiday, on the moors, on safari or in the rainforest. But spend just a few minutes outside your front door and you will soon see that we are surrounded by wildness. Flowers bloom in cracks in pavements, bumblebees slalom through the air, foxes skulk through the streets and swifts swoop overhead. We just need to open our eyes and see.

This little book is intended to help you to do that, every month of the year. The words are drawn from my annual almanacs, which chart the many ways in which the outside world changes with the seasons: the way the beehive shifts in purpose and energy from spring to summer to autumn; the mating flights of bluetits; the migrations of swifts, toads and Bewick swans. There is also a flower of the month, monthly visits to the ancient meadow from naturalist Kate Bradbury, as well as visits to the hedgerow, the pond and much more.

I have suggested ways to bring the outdoors in, with a nature table – they are not just for primary school! – and crafts such as an *Oesterierbaum*, or Easter egg tree, nature weaving and wand making. You'll find ways to mark the major turning points of the year – midsummer, midwinter and the equinoxes, and provided traditional songs and folklore about the natural world to find as many ways as possible to engage with the changing of the seasons indoors and out.

Times are tough for much of our flora and fauna, but connection leads to caretaking. The more we know what goes on in our skies, seas and soils, the more we love it. My hope is that in every month this book gives you the keys to finding out more about the wild world around you, and loving what you discover.

January

In the Ancient Meadow

In January, the ancient meadow sparkles with frost. The sward, cut in summer and grazed by cows, sheep or horses until the ground becomes too wet, sits close to the ground, with tufts of grass and tatty rosettes of wildflowers the only glimpses of its summer glory. Among them, caterpillars, beetles and other invertebrates hunker down to avoid the worst of the weather. The lime green chrysalises of speckled wood butterflies cling to the underside of stems, unnoticed by passing birds. Newts and toads share the space under logs with springtails, centipedes, woodlice and slugs. Beneath the surface, queen bumblebees hibernate, tucked into a waterproof, wax-lined cell. Yet, on mild days, earthworms may rise from beneath the frost layer to take old leaves and other detritus into the soil, leaving behind their tell-tale casts on the surface. The meadow lives, if only sporadically.

The sun hangs low in the sky and generates long shadows across the land. In landscapes with stone circles, such as Stonehenge, the shadows cast by standing stones stop the sun from melting any frost and snow on the surface. As the sun moves through the day, the patches of white gradually fade, although those closest to the stones may remain.

In the hoof-trodden mud, summer is a mere dream. Water pools in the prints left by grazing animals, and in these hoofprints, seeds of yellow rattle stick to the wet, frost-encrusted soil. Also known as 'meadow maker', yellow rattle is an annual plant that attaches itself to the root systems of grasses and partially parasitises them, reducing their growth and making conditions easier for wildflowers to thrive. The meadow might look dead and cold, but yellow rattle needs a long period of winter cold and wet to germinate. Without winter, the summer meadow is just not as pretty.

Kate Bradbury

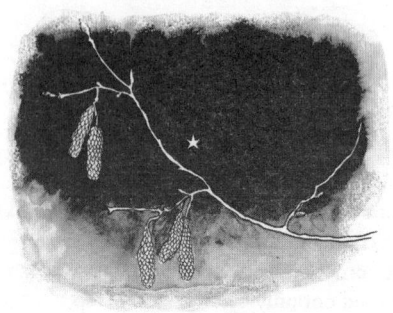

The Hedgerow in January

The hedgerow is asleep and so are its residents. There is some colour, from bramble leaves that still cling on in shades of yellow and purple, to the trails of cold-dulled ivy and the battered leaves of evergreen hart's-tongue fern, but mostly all is bare, brown and twiggy. Hedgehogs are rolled up at the hedgerow's base, spines out, under piles of leaves and damp earth; hoverflies are secreted into hollow stems; seven-spotted ladybirds pile together for warmth in sheltered nooks and rolled-up leaves. The hazel dormouse snoozes in deep hibernation in its nest at the base of the hedgerow, safe from the ravaging winds and snow above. Badgers in setts dug below the hedgerow aren't actually hibernating, but they sleep more during the winter, and change is happening while they sleep. Badgers mate all year round, but because they have 'delayed implantation' it is only during this winter lull that the fertilised eggs are implanted into the womb and the snoozing female becomes pregnant.

Ivy berries start to turn black and ripen this month and are pounced upon by hungry starlings, thrushes and wood pigeons, who also take the last few holly berries. Bluetits will find galls and break them open to get at the larvae inside. These are lean times. But there are signs of life even now. Hazel catkins are elongating, kicking the year off. Lesser celandine and snowdrops start to appear along the hedgerow bottom.

The Pond in January

Perhaps the single most useful thing one person can do to help wildlife is to build a pond in their garden or allotment. There was once a 'dew pond' (a shallow pond, usually man-made, replenished with water from the dew) in the corner of every field for livestock to drink from, and they would be used not only by cows and sheep but by amphibians, insects, small mammals and birds. Most have been drained or filled in and, of those that remain, around 80 per cent are thought to be polluted or degraded, mainly by the nitrogen and phosphorus from agricultural fertiliser.

Fortunately, garden ponds are insulated from many of the problems that countryside ponds face, and it is remarkably straightforward to create a pond that quickly becomes an intricate ecosystem supporting dozens of species. The phrase 'build it and they will come' could have been written for ponds: just make one, sit back and you will see. This year's almanac follows the year in a garden pond, and all the wonderful things that are happening above and below the surface.

There are few signs of life in the January pond. Many garden birds visit it to drink and wash, and mammals will stop by to drink: during mild, weather hedgehogs may even emerge from their sleep to take a drink. But other than that, all appears calm. Beneath the sometimes frozen surface, there is life, but it is at its lowest ebb. The bottom of the pond is full of decaying sticks and leaves, and nestled within it are the larvae of beetles and insects, and even adult water beetles, which will occasionally return briefly to the surface to take in air. Nymphs of caddisflies, dragonflies and mayflies are down there and create a kind of 'antifreeze' that prevents their bodies from freezing and their cells from rupturing. Dragonfly eggs nestled in the mud are in diapause, a type of hibernation that prevents them from hatching until the weather warms. Life is suspended, but not for long.

Garden Wildlife in January

Most garden wildlife is still hibernating, tucked up beneath leaves, in compost heaps or log piles, waiting out winter. But it's not uncommon to spot occasional signs of activity. A hedgehog might rouse itself from hibernation on mild evenings, in search of food, or you could spot a frog at the bottom of the pond. On dry, sunny days, red admiral butterflies can be found basking on a sunny wall, while honeybee hives buzz with the year's first tentative activity. But, for the most part, the garden is quiet, kept alive only by the activities of birds.

It might not look like a significant change, but the gradual lengthening of days after the winter solstice triggers birds into the beginnings of breeding activity. Signs will be subtle at first but you may spot magpies gathering sticks as a sort of trial run for the real deal in a few weeks' time, and tits entering and pecking at the holes of nest boxes. If you have a nest box and you haven't put it up yet, now's the time to do it.

It's amazing that birds have time to think about breeding when there are so few hours to find food. While day length is increasing slowly, small birds like tits and wrens are still spending most hours of daylight looking for food. These small birds have a high body temperature (around 40°C) and it takes a lot of calories to maintain that in cold weather.

Beneath the soil you might think nothing is happening, but plans are being made for summer: if temperatures are above 10°C, then tree roots of young trees will continue to grow, although less vigorously. This is the moment for them to put on growth that will sustain them in future weeks, months and years. They power away, unseen, while the rest of the garden sleeps.

Inside the Beehive in January

In the depths of winter, the main task for the beehive is keeping warm. There are very few flowers to visit anyway, and the colony stays inside the hive and survives on its stores of precious honey from the previous summer, or sometimes on sugar water provided by the beekeeper. To keep warm, the bees huddle closely together in a 'winter cluster' – a football-sized circle that spreads across several frames. The centre of the cluster can stay as warm as 38°C even when it is freezing outside. Bees on the outside of the cluster will stay almost motionless in cold weather, but those on the inside can move around a little in all but the coldest weather.

Look Out For

Fox Breeding Season

In cities and suburbs on January nights you may hear male foxes fighting, or the unearthly cries of female foxes during mating. This is fox breeding season, just a couple of weeks long, and litters of four or five cubs will be born in March. Cubs stay inside the den for six to eight weeks and will start tentatively venturing out to play, frolic and explore around June or July. They will be fully grown by September and finally leave the family in October to set up their own territories nearby.

Flower of the Month

Snowdrop

Latin name: *Galanthus nivalis* (*Galanthus* from the Greek *gala*, meaning 'milk', and *anthos*, meaning 'flower'; *nivalis* from Latin, meaning 'snowy', 'snow-covered', 'snow-like').
Common names: Mary's tapers, dingle-dangle, Candlemas bell. In France they are called *perce-neige*, which means snow-piercer.

Post-Christmas winter is the grimmest bit. No more hustle and bustle, present-giving and nonstop partying. Just the cold and the dark and the overwhelming feeling that you've slightly overdone it on several fronts. But step out into your garden on New Year's Day and there will be a reassuring sign that winter is moving on, and that spring will come: snowdrops, poking fresh green through the cold earth, and soon to produce their delicate, pure-white hanging droplets of flowers.

Snowdrops will collapse if frozen, but they quickly perk up again when temperatures rise, so don't worry: their leaves contain a sort of 'antifreeze' that prevents the cells from being damaged by frost. If you don't have any snowdrops in your garden, just after flowering is the time to remedy this by buying and planting them 'in the green', before the leaves have died down.

February

In the Ancient Meadow

There is more activity in the ancient meadow in February, though the ground is still hard and cold, or at least it should be. But there are stirrings for those who look for them: queen bumblebees flying low in search of a nest site, early magpies taking sticks and mud to build their dome-shaped nests. The odd fly will emerge from winter sleep and bask on a leaf or a stone in the weak sunshine. Mild days will see brand-new leaves and blades of grass pushing through the soil, and the first primroses and sweet violets might tentatively throw out a flower. In milder regions, frogs will rouse from hibernation and make their way to their breeding ponds, to spawn in great, vigorous parties. Look up on a sunny day and you may see skylarks yo-yoing above the meadow, their song echoing around the landscape.

On meadows with soil dry enough to support grazing livestock, these animals are now banished until autumn. Their grazing activity keeps the sward short and creates uneven surfaces for seeds to lodge and germinate. But if the animals remained at this time of year, the meadow wouldn't grow. From now, the plants can bulk up unencumbered, except for the gentle attentions of deer and rabbits, who usually cause little damage to the grassland. Evergreen rosettes can leaf up before sending out a flower, while annuals may germinate and herbaceous perennials throw up the first shoots of spring.

In forgotten hoofprints, the yellow rattle germinates, sending up two tiny embryonic leaves from which dark green, serrated leaves with purple blotches follow. They're hard to spot in the tufts of grass but they will steadily put on growth from now, eventually forming long, dark, toothed leaves from black-spotted stems. In just a few weeks they, and all the wildflowers they support, will be flowering.

Kate Bradbury

Nature Table

An Arrangement for February

Try to include some signs of the earth turning, and the new bulbs starting to shoot. Snowdrops are symbols of purity, optimism and hope, and as such are closely associated with Candlemas on 2nd February, which is the only day they can be brought into the house without incurring bad luck. A lovely way to enjoy them is to dig up a little clump in flower and pot it temporarily into a terracotta pot, topped with moss, in which case they are still half outdoors, really.

Your table this month might include:
- White candles for St Brigid and Candlemas
- A St Brigid's cross made of reeds for St Brigid's day
- Snowdrops
- A little vase of winter honeysuckle
- Lichened bark
- Feathers
- Pebbles

It is still dark enough in the mornings to light a candle, but it won't be so for long. Try to enjoy these dark and cosy moments in the year before they have passed, rather than wishing them away too fast. St Brigid is the patron saint of many things,rat including craft and poetry, so you might include a little piece of something you have made yourself, such as some embroidery or crochet, or even a poem.

Migration of the Month

Toad

This month's migration is perhaps not the most epic of our journeys, and the mode of travel is hardly the most elegant, but it is happening almost under our feet, and is as perilous and fraught with danger as any globetrotting trek. Throughout this month, toads will start to stir, having been firmly tucked away until now in their winter hibernacula (where they hibernate) in the mud at the bottom of ponds, under piles of leaves or dug deep down in the ground below the frost line.

Although they have evolved the ability to live their entire lives on dry land, toads must have water to breed. By the end of the month, they will be on the move, the males setting out first, plodding rather than hopping towards the ponds where they were born. They have incredible homing instincts and will travel for several miles, moving at night to avoid the sun, steadfastly making their way over every obstacle. Or at least attempting to. There is clearly great danger in crossing roads by night at toad's pace, and every year there are a large number of casualties, sometimes mitigated by 'toad patrols'. (Look for one to join locally and help to usher toads safely through the night.) If you see 'toads crossing' signs when driving, slow right down to toad-dodging speed. Intensive agriculture and the loss of many dew ponds have had a big impact on toad populations, but garden ponds have come to the rescue – as often as not it is now these ponds that toads migrate towards in this great annual amphibian ramble.

The only thing that eases the male toad's tricky passage is if he chances upon a female toad, in which case he won't hesitate to climb upon her back and piggyback a lift the rest of the way. Once their home pond is reached, the coupled-up pair will breed – or if a female arrives alone, then a load of males will jump on her to form a 'toad ball', all trying their luck. Long strings of eggs encased in jelly are laid right across the pond. After 14 days, the jelly disintegrates and the tadpoles drop into the water to begin life in their own home pond.

Folk Song of the Month

'Green Grows the Laurel'

Traditional, arr. Richard Barnard

This song for Valentine's Day is about losing a lover and wanting them back, and it references violets, February's birth flower. The song employs the Victorian idea of the 'language of flowers', with violets representing loyalty and faithfulness. The melody is close to a Romani version collected in Hampshire in the 1900s.

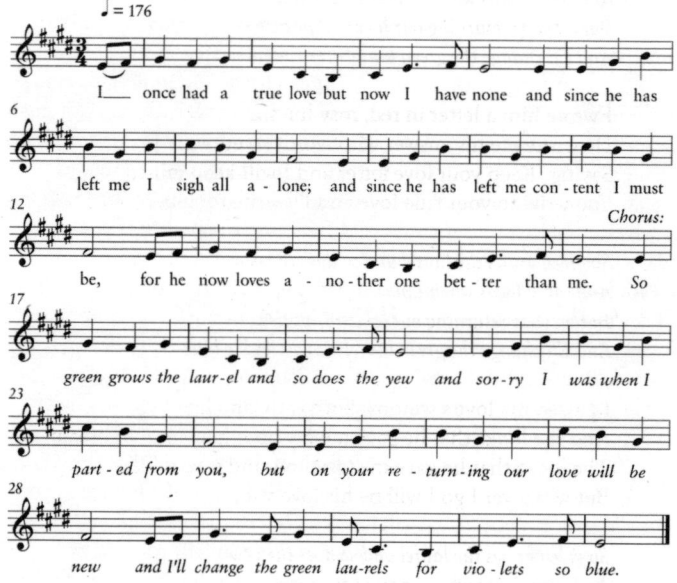

I once had a true love but now I have none
And since he has left me I sigh all alone;
And since he has left me content I must be,
For he now loves another one better than me.

So green grows the laurel and so does the yew
And sorry I was when I parted from you,
But on your returning our love will be new
And I'll change the green laurels for violets so blue.

I wrote him a letter in red, rosy lines.
He wrote me his answer with words so entwined
Saying, 'Keep your love letter and I will keep mine,
You write to your true love and I'll write to mine.'

So green grows the laurel and so does the yew
And sorry I was when I parted from you,
But on your returning our love will be new
And I'll change the green laurels for violets so blue.

I passed my love's window both early and late
And the looks that he gave me my poor heart would break;
The looks that he gave me ten thousand would kill,
But wherever I go I will be his love still.

So green grows the laurel and so does the yew
And sorry I was when I parted from you,
But on your returning our love will be new
And I'll change the green laurels for violets so blue.

The Hedgerow in February

Along the base of the hedgerow comes a smattering of hopeful yellow and white this month: lesser celandine, winter aconite, primroses and snowdrops appear, and there will also be a few purple dog violets in the mix if you're lucky. Wood anemones start into flower this month. They are an indicator species for ancient woodland so, if you spot them, you know that you are dealing with a remnant of a very old piece of woodland indeed, possibly a thousand years old or more.

On the warm days this month it can suddenly feel like spring is here: the first butterflies – pale yellow-green brimstones – emerge and flit about the flowers in the weak sun, having overwintered in nooks and crannies in the hedge. Queen buff-tailed and early bumblebees emerge from the holes in the ground where they have spent the winter, visiting flowers to drink nectar and strengthen up after winter. Each queen searches for an underground nest site under tussocky grass, and when she has chosen one, she visits the hazel catkins to collect pollen. Back in the nest she mixes the pollen with wax from her body and lays her first brood onto it.

A few of the black berries of the wild privet bushes cling on, but this is a lean time for foraging, so most creatures are still conserving their energy, sleeping or hibernating. Deer may creep along the hedge line, using it for shelter, protection and grazing. It is time for a spring-clean in the badger setts below the hedge, with the badgers pulling out the old winter bedding and dragging in fresh beds of dried bracken and leaves.

Winter Rainbows

To spot a rainbow, all you need is sunshine and showers, your back to the sun and the rainstorm ahead of you. The effect is created when thousands of raindrops refract white light into the full spectrum. Bold, bright, colourful rainbows mean big raindrops. They can be easier to spot in autumn, winter and spring because of the angle of the sun: the lower the sun is to the horizon, the more of the rainbow we see. There is no possibility of a sighting once the sun is more than 42 degrees above the horizon. High summer suns towards the middle of the day bring arcs so shallow that they are lost along or below the horizon, while low winter suns (or morning or evening suns in summer) bring dramatically arched arcs.

Flower of the Month

Sweet Violet

Latin name: *Viola odorata* (*Viola* from the Latin for the colour violet; *odorata* from the Latin for 'sweet smelling').
Common names: wood violet, English violet, florist's violet, lesbian flower.

We will be told plenty of times this month that violets are blue, when they are clearly violet: just like orange, the colour was named after the thing. They are in flower this month, very much unlike roses (which are often red), but sadly they are rarely given as valentines despite the fact that they have traditionally been understood to be a romantic token, meaning 'My thoughts are occupied with love' in the Victorian language of flowers. They are particularly associated with lesbian love and were known in 1920s New York as the 'lesbian flower', possibly because of a poem by Sappho in which she describes herself and her lover wearing violets: 'If you forget me, think of our gifts to Aphrodite and all the loveliness that we shared, all the violet tiaras, braided rosebuds, dill and crocus twined around your young neck.'

There are other violets around but you can identify sweet violet by its strong perfumed scent. They make a wonderful and medicinal syrup, if you can gather enough. Home is in damp and semi-shady spots, peeking out from under hedgerows and spread across woodland floors, but they are also easy to cultivate in similar spots in gardens. Track down seed from specialist suppliers, and sow some future love tokens of your own now.

Inside the Beehive in February

February can be very cold, and in these conditions the colony is still using all of its energy to keep warm and stay alive. But there are a few flowers out now, and in mild winters the bees will start to make brief forays to visit snowdrops and crocuses in sunny spots, and to collect some early pollen, before quickly returning to the warmth of the hive. They also use these short early flights to clean themselves after a winter indoors. In mild winters, the queen may lay a few eggs in February, to get ahead, but the larvae must be kept warm in the very centre of the cluster.

Look Out For

Bluetit Display Flights

Male bluetits start singing heartily in February, impressing potential mates that they have made it through winter and with energy to spare. If you are lucky, you may also spot one making odd display flights, which is all part of the show: he will utter a brief, trembling trill before setting off in a parachuting glide towards a female's chosen nest site, or he might beat his wings shallowly and rapidly, moving between nearby perches. Despite the bravado, this is a tough time for these birds. They will have been weakened by winter, and natural food sources are now very low as winter drags on. Putting out high-fat foods such as sunflower seeds, peanuts, grated suet or fat balls can help them make it through cold nights. Clean, non-frozen water is a life-saver now, too.

March

In the Ancient Meadow

There is more life to the ancient meadow with every passing day. It's still green and low-growing, much like a lawn, but look closely and you will see the bulking of leaves and the first, tentative nibbles of caterpillars. On chalk grassland, spotted orchids throw up rosettes of green leaves with purple-brown spots. They won't flower until next month but other low-growing plants will, including coltsfoot, dandelions, cowslips and, on wetter meadows, marsh marigold. These are visited by pollinators: early bumblebees are joined by solitary hairy-footed flower bees and the first of the year's butterflies, hoverflies and strange-looking bee-flies, which look like bees but hover like flies, gathering around spring flowers with their long proboscises exposed.

On lowland meadows, brown hares shelter during the day, emerging at dusk to nibble grass shoots for sustenance. They bear a passing resemblance to rabbits but are bigger and stronger-looking and have longer ears and longer hind legs. They are mainly solitary, but at this time of year they are more likely in pairs or small groups, the female often fending off one or more amorous males. If you visit a lowland meadow at dawn or dusk, you may be lucky enough to observe a 'boxing' display, where the male chases a female and she fends him off by appearing to 'box' with him. This behaviour has given hares a reputation for being mad and is the source of the expression 'mad as a March hare'.

Eventually they do mate. The female can rear up to four litters a year, each with two to four young, known as leverets. Leverets are born with their eyes open and a full body of brown fur. Their mother leaves them in or near a small depression in the ground known as a 'form', where they hunker down to avoid the attentions of foxes. At sunset she returns to feed them.

Kate Bradbury

The Vernal / Spring Equinox

The earth takes 24 hours to rotate on its axis, with half of the earth in shadow (night) and half in light (day). It does this on an angle of 23.4 degrees known as the 'axial tilt', and it is this angle that is responsible for our seasons, because as well as rotating on its own axis, the earth also orbits the sun, taking a year to do so. During this time the axial tilt stays constant, and so, as the earth moves around the sun, different parts receive greater or smaller amounts of sun.

When the earth is at the point where the North Pole is leaning towards the sun, we have reached the northern hemisphere's summer solstice, and the southern hemisphere's winter solstice. When the earth moves around to the other side of the sun, so that the South Pole is tilted towards the sun, then the southern hemisphere has its summer solstice and the northern hemisphere has its winter solstice. The equinoxes, in spring and autumn, occur at the halfway points between these moments. The axis of the earth at these times is side-on to the sun, which means that – momentarily – no hemisphere is favoured. Day and night are roughly even, all over the world, from tropical Colombia at the equator to icy Lapland in the Arctic Circle. The exact moment of the equinox is when the sun is directly overhead at the equator.

Common wisdom has it that, at the equinox, day and night are exactly the same length, but this is not quite true. It would be correct if sunrise and sunset were measured from the moment that the centre of the sun rises over or sinks below the horizon, but we measure them from the moment the top edge appears or disappears. Thus, the equinox day is a little longer than its night and its length varies slightly through the world. In spring, 'equilux', which is when day and night are exactly the same length, occurs a few days before the equinox.

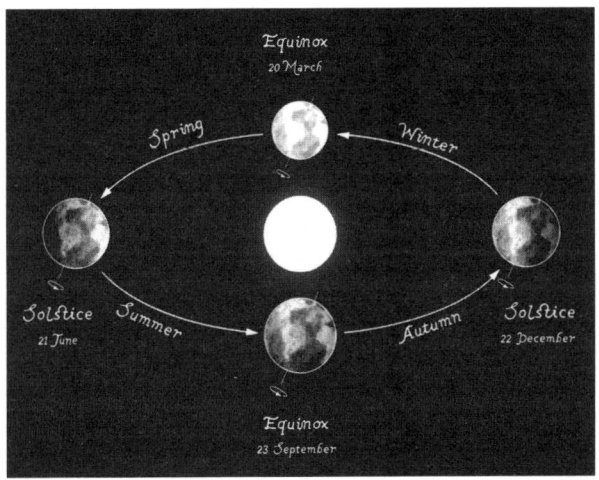

Naming of the Equinox

The word 'equinox' is derived from two Latin words, *aequus* 'equal' and *nox* 'night'. The spring equinox is sometimes called the vernal equinox, the word vernal being a 16th-century English word derived from the Latin *vernalis*, which itself is derived from the Latin word for spring, *ver*. The Welsh name for the spring solstice is Alban Eilir, *albann* meaning 'quarter year' and *eilir* meaning 'spring'. In Scottish Gaelic it is called *co-fhad-thrath an earraiche* and in Irish Gaelic *conoct an earraiche*. Spring equinox is called Ostara by modern Wiccans, Druids and Pagans, after the Germanic goddess Eostre, who is associated with the east and dawn.

Garden and Weather Folklore

We don't want warm weather too soon, according to weather lore: 'When the apple blooms in March, for the fruit you'll search.' Watch out for a spell of cold weather at the end of the month that coincides with the blackthorn blossom and is known as a 'blackthorn winter'. Also be wary on 29th, 30th and 31st March, as these are the 'borrowed days', believed in Irish custom to have been borrowed from April. They are said to bring about a wintry relapse. Snowfall this month is called a 'lambing storm', and is expected – or perhaps hoped – to be brief.

Inside the Beehive in March

As the weather warms and the days lengthen, activity within the hive increases. Lots of worker bees – non-reproducing female bees that do most of the work of the hive – must be raised to replace the bees that have died over winter, and so the queen starts laying lots of eggs into brood cells that are situated in the centre of the frame and capped with a small dome of yellowy wax. There are more forays out of the hive to seek early bloomers – wood anemone, sweet violets, blackthorn, pussy willow and goat willow – and hopefully return with pollen baskets laden. This month is essential to replenish the hive's stores after the long winter: a wet and cold spring with few flowers can be disastrous, but a mild spell now will set the colony up for a bumper summer.

Look Out For

Hedgehogs Coming Out of Hibernation

Hedgehogs emerge from hibernation this month, hungry, thirsty and disorientated: they will have lost a third of their body weight over winter and need to replenish it fast, ready for breeding season. Make a hedgehog feeding station so that they can eat and drink away from predators such as foxes and badgers. Cut a 12–15cm square hole in one end of a large plastic storage box with a lid, covering the sharp edges with duct tape. Place newspaper in the box, and then place a bowl each of water and a meat-based cat food (chicken is best – no fish) at the end farthest from the hole. Tuck the box under a hedge or into a border. Put a weight such as a brick on the lid so it doesn't come off. You can make a feeding station even if you have never seen a hedgehog in your garden: they are hard to spot even if they are there, and are also in extreme decline, so worth taking a punt on.

Garden Craft

Oesterierbaum, or Easter Egg Tree

In Germany and Austria at Eastertide, blossom trees are decorated with hundreds of small Easter egg decorations, hung from ribbons. Some people choose to decorate trees outdoors, while others bring a branch indoors. The warmth indoors will encourage the buds to begin to grow and the blossom to bloom.

You will need:
- A branch – cherry, magnolia or blackthorn blossom, corkscrew hazel or pussy willow work particularly well
- A large narrow-necked vase filled with water
- Pebbles
- Hanging Easter egg decorations, small pompoms in pastel colours trimmed into egg shapes and/or fluffy chicks
- Pastel-coloured 3mm-wide ribbon
- A large-eyed needle

Place your branch in the vase (placing pebbles in the bottom of the vase to hold the branch upright if necessary). Use a large-eyed needle to thread lengths of ribbon through the eggs, pompoms and/or chicks, then hang the decorations from the branches using the ribbons.

Garden Wildlife in March

Things are suddenly very busy in our gardens. Bird nesting proceeds apace, although this depends on temperature, food and the condition of the birds themselves. Winter is a difficult time for them, and some will be in better shape than others. Those nesting now tend to be older and more experienced, while the younger birds will need another few weeks before they're in prime breeding condition.

Ponds bubble with mating amphibians. Frogs in the southwest start spawning first, with those further north and east joining the party as temperatures increase. Fertilisation is external, with the male frog clasping onto the back of the female in a position called amplexus. Spawn is laid in clumps and eaten by many species, including dragonfly larvae, newts and birds. If you think you have too much frogspawn in your pond, you haven't – most of it will be eaten by predators.

Meanwhile hedgehogs are coming out of hibernation and are hungry. They're known for eating slugs and snails but they're much more likely to feast on caterpillars, beetles and earthworms. Wilder gardens, with plenty of leaf litter, a compost heap, areas of long grass and a log pile, will have the greatest number of invertebrates for hedgehogs to eat.

If you live near the coast, keep an eye out for migrating birds, which can be found refuelling in gardens, as pitstops on their way to or from, their destination. At this time of year, redwings and fieldfares are starting to leave the UK for Scandinavia and Russia. Listen out for the 'tseep' of redwings flying overhead, and the 'football rattle' sound of fieldfares. They may spend a few days in gardens, feeding, before their long journey back to their mating grounds, and will benefit from any berries or windfall fruit you have left.

Meanwhile chiffchaffs are arriving, again spending a few days in coastal gardens before heading inland. Notice them teasing the first of the year's aphids off your roses, and listen for their early calls of 'chiff chaff' within a growing dawn chorus.

Migration of the Month

Bewick's Swan

While we mostly see returnees at this time of year – creatures that have spent winter somewhere warmer – the hardy and elegant Bewick's swans are about to leave us. These are the smallest swans that visit our islands, the adults pure white with a yellow and black bill and the juveniles grey with a soft pink bill. Their call is gentle and musical, markedly different from the comedy honk of whooper swans. Bewick's swans use their voices often, making a range of different noises for different purposes: pre-flight, while flying, to locate each other, to threaten, to mark out territory and undoubtedly much more.

There are three distinct groups of Bewick's swans, and those that overwinter in the United Kingdom and Ireland are the northwest European population. In summer, they breed on moss-lichen tundra near shallow pools and lakes to the west of the Ural Mountains in the Russian Arctic. Cold, yes, but relatively predator-free and with almost constant daylight for foraging. But winter is a different matter. In comparison with the Arctic, our winter weather is a luxury. The birds overwinter on our freshwater wetlands – reedbeds, wet grasslands, fens and bogs – and frequent farmland by day to pick over the leavings of last year's crops, feasting on sugar beet, potatoes and wheat stubble before returning to the water to roost at night.

Bewick's swans mate for life – one pair returned to Slimbridge Wetland Centre in Gloucestershire every year for 19 years, bringing 29 cygnets. They travel in family groups, teaching the cygnets the route, and if separated will seek each other out and perform a joyful dance on reuniting. Extended family groups of parents, siblings and even grandchildren will honk joyfully when they find themselves together. Now that winter is over, it is time for them to group together and head off to their breeding grounds. It is a long and treacherous journey of up to 5,600km, with hunters, power lines and predators to avoid. Hopefully it will be a successful one this year and the Bewick's families will be reunited again next winter.

A Song for March

'The Oxen Ploughing'

Traditional, arr. Richard Barnard

The Plough Moon is one of the old names for March's moon, presumably because there was lots of ploughing to do before sowing the year's corn. This is also one of the best times to see the Plough, the cluster of stars also known as the Big Dipper, in the sky. One saying goes 'spring up, fall down' – in spring and summer the Plough is high in the sky, while in autumn and winter it sweeps lower, closer to the horizon.

It is likely that, for thousands of years, oxen pulled the original ploughs. They are generally slower beasts than horses (which were used later) and need a lot of chivvying along. This song was collected by Sabine Baring-Gould in Cornwall in 1906.

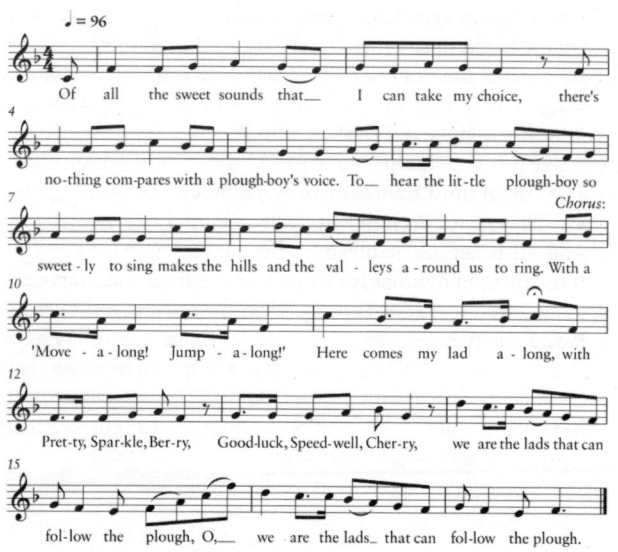

Of all the sweet sounds that I can take my choice,
There's nothing compares with a ploughboy's voice.
To hear the little ploughboy so sweetly to sing
Makes the hills and the valleys around us to ring.

With a 'Move along! Jump along!'
Here comes my lad along,
With Pretty, Sparkle, Berry,
Good luck, Speedwell, Cherry,
We are the lads that can follow the plough, O,
We are the lads that can follow the plough.

In the heat of the day there is little we can do!
We lay by our oxen for an hour or two,
On the banks of sweet violets where we take our rest,
Where cool breezes blow all around us so fresh.

Repeat chorus

The farmer must have corn, or else he cannot sow;
The miller with his mill wheel's an idle man also,
And the baker has no bread for the poor to provide;
If the ploughboy stops his ploughing, we should all starve alive.

Repeat chorus

Bird of the Month

Skylark

This is a wonderful time to go out into the countryside and see if you can spot a skylark. Chances are, though, that you will hear one first, and when you see it the bird will be a mere speck, high above your head. Male skylarks rise vertically up into the air and then hover there, fluttering their wings to remain stationary. They stay at 50–200m high for up to an hour, singing their hearts out across the meadows, salt marshes, heath and farmland that they most often inhabit. The song is complex and varied, containing much mimicry of other birds – the songs of linnets, corn buntings, curlews and redshanks can all get thrown into the glorious mix, depending on the habitat that each skylark inhabits. Eventually they make a gliding, parachuting flight back down to the ground. Skylarks sing like this almost all year round. The song has different purposes throughout the year but in the spring it is to attract a mate.

Once they pair up, skylarks go to the other extreme and make their cup-shaped grass nests directly on the ground. Sadly, these are very susceptible to predators, which may partly account for the extreme decline in the birds' numbers. Skylark pairs will lay several broods of eggs through the season. The hatchlings leave the nest before they can fly, after just eight to ten days, but they stay nearby and continue to be fed by the parents for a further ten days.

The skylark is an unremarkable-looking bird, a little smaller than a starling, with soft brown markings on the head and back and a pale brown breast. The males and females are very similar. You are most likely to spot one by its behaviour and song. Larks have been much celebrated in poetry and music, and their song is traditionally associated with daybreak.

The Hedgerow in March

The hedgerow starts to wake up this month. Muntjac deer may browse and nibble on the new green hedge growth and the lemony sorrel at the base. Pussy willow catkins burst open and clouds of blackthorn blossom appear, the flowers white with long yellow stamens against the still-bare spiky black stems. Peacock, small tortoiseshell and comma butterflies emerge and feed on the pollen, along with queen white-tailed bumblebees, just out of hibernation. Hedgehogs are also waking up to snuffle between the clumps of wild daffodils, searching for slugs on which to fatten themselves up. The spring usher, the early moth and the March moth might be seen in the evenings, and bats – which have been in a state of dormancy all winter and have now reached the end of their fat reserves – start to make short, flitting flights around the hedgerows in search of the moths.

New life is emerging as the weather is at its most unpredictable, meaning the shelter the hedgerow provides is crucial. For many birds, this is nest-building time. Female blackbirds build their sturdy nests low in the hedgerow, while female robins build a dome-shaped nest from grass, leaves and moss on which they lay their first batch of pale, speckled eggs. Wrens do things a little differently: the male builds a succession of nests and invites the female to choose one, which she then lines with feathers. Pairs of song thrushes build their nests together from dry grass and leaves, lining the insides with mud. Linnets are building their nests, too. These are cup-shaped and lined with moss and feathers. Grey partridges scrape indentations in the ground at the base of the hedgerow and line it with leaves and grasses ready to hold their precious eggs.

SPRING HEDGEROW FLOWERS

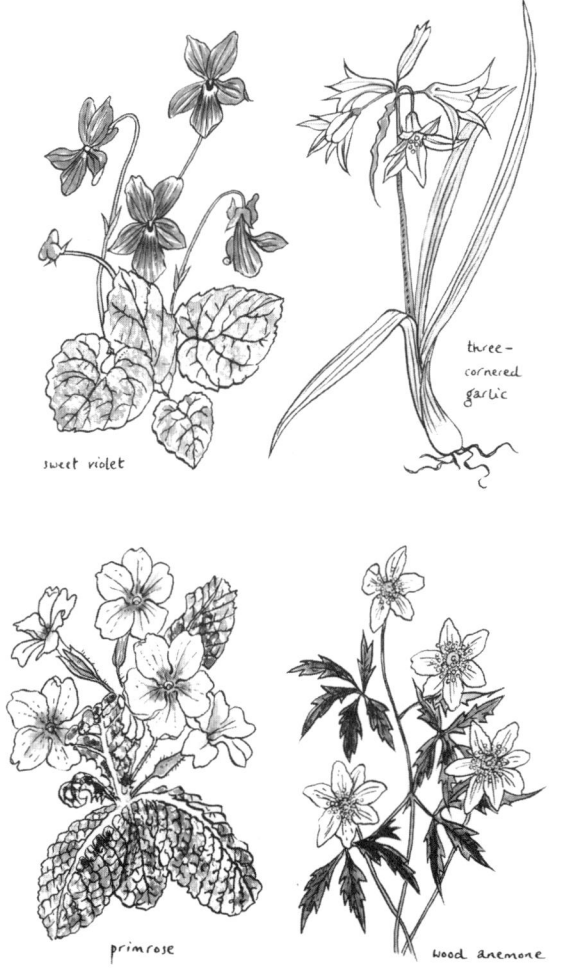

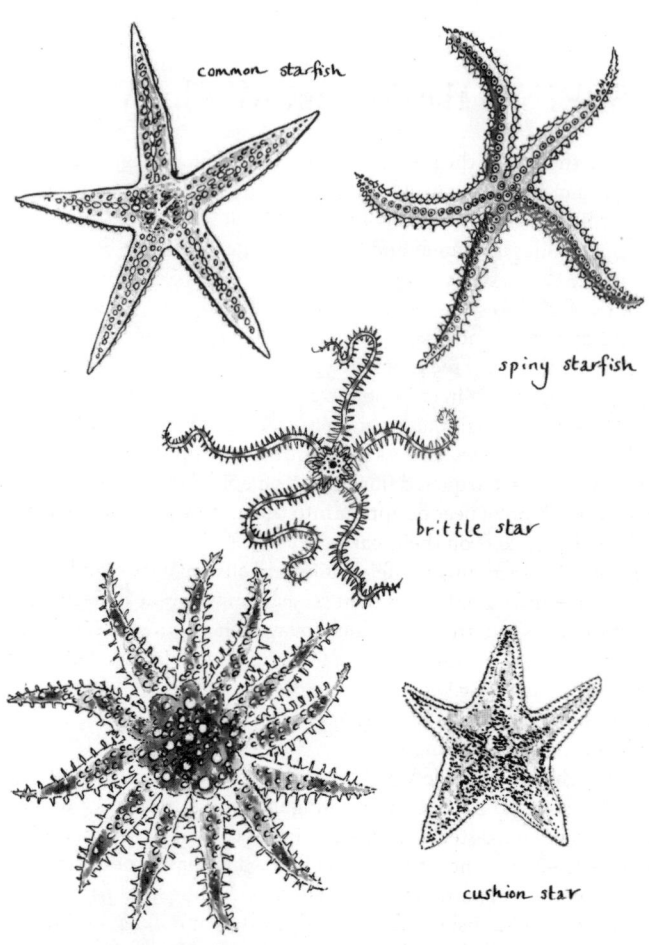

April

In the Ancient Meadow

In April, the first of the meadow grasses flower, including sweet vernal grass and meadow foxtail. The height of the grass is now sufficient for small rodents such as short-tailed field voles to traverse the meadow through a series of tunnels and burrows in the long grass. Feeding both day and night on seeds and grass stems, field voles attract the attention of birds of prey: kestrels and owls hover over grassland, homing in on the tiniest movement or sound from a vole in the grass. Watch awhile and eventually you'll see them dive down, where they will grab the unsuspecting rodent in their powerful claws, before swooping back into the sky with their quarry, and returning to a perch to eat it.

On wetter meadows, snake's head fritillaries send up their beautiful cream-and-wine-chequered flowers, which bob in the breeze as the first worker bumblebees disappear into them, stowing the pollen in tight pollen baskets on their rear legs.

Everything is coming to life all at once: house sparrows land on grass stems and strip them of their seeds, common blue butterflies scout for bird's foot trefoil in which to lay their eggs. On the ground, adders bask in the spring sunshine to warm their cold-blooded bodies, while solitary mining bees delve into patches of bare soil, some making volcano-like mounds in huge aggregations, as evidence of their enthusiastic nest-building.

In the thatch, speckled wood butterfly caterpillars emerge and begin eating grasses, before metamorphosing into chrysalises, stuck to the undersides of grass stems. Overwintering as caterpillars or chrysalises, those who entered the latter stage before winter have a head start, and will be on the wing now, sheltering close by. Males patrol patches of grass in dappled sunshine, fighting off rivals by spiralling into the sky. If a female likes the look of a male, she will drop down and mate with him, before finding more grasses to lay her eggs on.

Kate Bradbury

Garden and Weather Folklore

'If it thunders on All Fools' Day, it brings good crops of corn and hay.' This particular old saying about the weather on April Fools' Day might have a little science behind it. Thunderstorms only occur when warm air rises from heated ground, forming highly charged cumulonimbus clouds that produce thunder and lightning. Ground that is warm enough for thunderstorms at this moment in the year suggests an early spring, and the start of a good growing season.

Sayings about St George's Day on the 23rd claim that this is the day green growth begins. An old Estonian adage says, 'With his key George makes the grass grow.' In Lithuanian tradition, George is the keeper of the keys to summer and is asked to make the grass grow and to disperse the clouds.

Something to look out for this month is the budding of the trees. The old saying, 'Oak before ash, in for a splash; ash before oak, in for a soak' suggests that the weather for the coming summer will be drier if oak comes into leaf first.

The Hedgerow in April

Last month a few buds appeared over the dark brown twigginess of the hedgerow, but during the showery and ever-warming month of April the hazel, blackthorn and hawthorn start to properly green up. They are joined by a general unfurling and uncurling of soft shield fern, western polypody, male fern and hart's-tongue fern, all along the damp hedge bottom. And here comes the blossom in abundance: wild cherry, elder and the start of the great hawthorn blooming, now visited by green-veined white, holly blue, orange tip and speckled wood butterflies, all starting to emerge from winter chrysalises. Northern hedgerows will see sweet cicely, too. Red-tailed bumblebee queens are visiting all of the flowers – which now include jack-by-the-hedge, starry white greater stitchwort and dog violet, and the first of the bluebells – to fuel up after they emerge from their winter hibernation underground.

By night, badger cubs start to explore around the entrance to their sett, staying close to their mother. Bank voles are producing their first litters of the season from their grass-lined nests beneath the roots. Stoats produce one litter per year around now, kept cosy during the unpredictable spring weather in their fur-lined burrows.

Pairs of chaffinches have started building their nests together, lining them with softest moss, wool and feathers so that the female can lay three to six pale eggs splotched with brownish red. Greenfinches are taking much less fastidious care, making a rough-and-ready nest in dense, bushy parts of the hedgerow in which to raise their own broods.

The Pond in April

There is an explosion of green here in April, as frogbit, hornwort, water soldiers and broad-leaved pondweed rise up from the mud at the bottom, reach the surface and spread their leaves, ready to make the most of the warmth and daylight. Water lilies do the same, spreading their pads across the surface, providing little islands for any creatures needing a rest from all of their activity.

And there are plenty which do. We are into the main breeding season now, and every creature in the garden has a use to make of the pond and its surroundings. Swallows and house martins collect mud from the edges to build their nests. Moths, leaf miners and aphids lay their eggs on the leaves around the pond. Sparrows swoop in and take the aphids and caterpillars for their own babies, as well as bathing and drinking at the edges. Yellow flag iris and marsh marigold are in flower, and the bees visit them for pollen and nectar. When they get weary, they might rest on a lily pad and take a sip of pond water before continuing on with their work. The hatched tadpoles have now started to grow legs, and they switch from being vegetarian to eating dead insects from the water's surface. This is a great time for pond-dipping. A bucketful of water will be alive with water boatmen, pond snails and dragonfly larvae.

There are three newts native to the UK – the smooth newt (by far the most common), the palmate newt and the great crested newt. Only smooth newts are native to Ireland. Newts are secretive breeders, choosing deeper ponds, and carrying out most of their breeding by night. Shine a torch into your night-time pond to try to spot one. They begin breeding some time in April and continue for up to six weeks. In the run-up to breeding, the male puts on a show, brightening his colours, extending the crest that runs along his back, and then performing a ritualistic dance, swishing, fanning and whipping his tail. When the female accepts him, he will touch her with his tail to transfer sperm. The female wraps each individual fertilised egg in a leaf, laying up to 600 between now and July.

Inside the Beehive in April

The brood of new worker-bee larvae must be kept warm no matter how cold it becomes outside, and 'nurse' bees may dip into the last of the winter honey stores from the wax-capped cells along the top of the frame to produce body heat. When these crucial first worker bees of the year chew their way out of their cells, they go straight to work visiting wild cherry blossom, cowslips, dandelions, clover and the first apple blossom and bluebells, and starting the year's labour. But honey making is not the main task just yet. First, the workers collect nectar for energy (stored in glistening open cells just below the capped winter honey) and pollen for protein (creating multicoloured and multi-textured cells as varied as the flowers they have visited, just below the pollen cells) to feed and fuel the fast-expanding colony.

Look Out For

Brimstone Butterflies

The first butterflies of the year are very often brimstone butterflies, the females palest green and the males butter yellow. It is thought that the word butterfly is derived from 'butter-coloured fly' after the male of this species. They are so early because they hibernate through winter as adults in outbuildings, cracks in stone walls and hollows in trees rather than overwintering as pupae. This is so that they can emerge as soon as the weather warms, though it can leave them vulnerable to early emergence during mild spells or to late cold snaps. Brimstone is another word for sulphur, which is the colour of the wings.

Flower of the Month

Bluebell

Latin name: *Hyacinthoides non-scripta* (*Hyacinthoides* from the Latin, meaning 'like a hyacinth'; *non-scripta*, which is Latin for 'not written'. This relates to the mythical hyacinth of Greek legend created from the blood of dying Hyacinthus and written on in tears by his lover Apollo. So the non-scripta part of the name is a way of saying 'and it's not that hyacinth either'.)
Common names: English bluebell, wild hyacinth, fairy flower, bell bottle, wood bell.

Bluebell woods produce one of the great natural spectacles of the British Isles this month and next. Exact timing depends on where you are and how cold it has been, but start planning yourself a woodland walk. This is the woodland floor grabbing its moment in the brief period between winter ending and the canopy filling out and blocking light: a temporal niche filled with a sea of purple-blue. The most stunning shows will be under the canopies that cast the densest summer shade, as this suppresses competing ground cover and lets the bluebells dominate. Bluebells are indicator species for ancient woodland, so their presence suggests that a wood dates back to at least 1600.

You can buy bulbs from a reputable supplier in autumn – it is illegal to lift them from the ground – but do consider if your efforts will really rival the sight of a bluebell wood in full purple haze, or if this one is best left to nature.

A Song for Spring
'When Spring Comes In'

Traditional

This song is a simple and joyful celebration of this lovely moment in the year, when winter is finally relinquishing its grip.

When spring comes in the birds do sing the lambs do skip and the bells do ring, While we

en-joy their glor - ious charm so

no-ble and so gay oh the prim-rose blooms and the cow slip too the vi-olets in their sweet

re-tire, the ro - ses shi - ning through the briar and the daff-o-downdillies that we ad-mire will

die and fade a - way.

Young men and maidens will be seen,
On mountains high and meadows green,
They will talk of love and sport and play,
While these young lambs do skip away.
At night they homeward wend their way,
When evening stars appear.

Oh the primrose blooms and the cowslip too,
The violets in their sweet retire, the roses shining through the briar,
And the daffadowndillies that we admire will die and fade away.

The dairymaid to milking goes, her
blooming cheeks as red as a rose,
She carries her pail all on her arm so cheerful and so gay,
She milks, she sings and the valleys ring,
The small birds on the branches there
sit listening to this lovely fair.
For she is her master's trust and care, she is the ploughman's joy.

Oh the primrose blooms and the cowslip too,
The violets in their sweet retire, the roses shining through the briar,
And the daffadowndillies that we admire will die and fade away.

May

In the Ancient Meadow

The May meadow dances in the breeze, its grasses and flowers tall enough to finally bring movement and life to the landscape. From now, the space becomes more colourful, with early purple orchids and small annuals such as forget-me-nots complementing the yellow palette of primroses and cowslips. On wetter meadows, ragged robin and cuckoo flower flourish, visited, perhaps, by the first of the year's orange-tip butterflies. In wood meadows, where some or all of the meadow lies beneath trees and shrubs, flowers of hawthorn take centre stage, with a multitude of pollinators clamouring to feed from them. Beneath them the pinks of shade-tolerant red campion and cranesbill vie for attention.

Above the meadow, skylarks dance, their song rising as they climb into the sky. These inconspicuous brown birds nest on the ground in short grass and may take advantage of the shorter height of the spring meadow to lay eggs for their first brood, before the vegetation becomes too tall for further nesting attempts. Like hares in their forms, the brown skylarks are well camouflaged in the spring meadow, although predation from foxes is high.

On rougher grassland and moorland, meadow pipits perform a fluttering, or 'parachuting', display flight. Like the skylark, they nest on the ground, often in a tussock of grass on a slope. The female builds the nest with grass and hair, and lays four or five eggs. However, only one may survive: meadow pipits are often the unwitting foster parents of cuckoo chicks, whose mother lays a single egg in the unsuspecting meadow pipit's nest. After hatching, the cuckoo pushes out the meadow pipit chicks and takes all of the food for itself. It soon grows bigger than its new parents but they continue to feed it for around two weeks, until the cuckoo is ready to fledge.

Kate Bradbury

The Hedgerow in May

This month the vibrant lime green of the hedgerow is all but eclipsed by white froth. Hawthorn – the plant that dominates our hedgerows – is in explosive, pure white flower, but then so are cow parsley, wayfaring tree and elder. It's a symphony of white. There is vibrant colour to be found, too, though. Bluebells are at their peak, and they are joined by pink herb Robert, acid-green Alexanders, purple dog violets and fat golden dandelions all along the hedgerow bottom. Large cabbage white, orange tip and holly blue butterflies visit them for nectar, while the overwintering population of red admiral butterflies is bolstered this month by a great influx of migrants fluttering over from mainland Europe. They mate and lay their eggs on the tips of the nettle leaves. Magpie moths are emerging, taking to the wing, and laying eggs. Their larvae feast on young hawthorn leaves.

Badger cubs come out and explore, sometimes even in the daytime. May is the beginning of the main hedgehog rutting season, though some will have started in April. Pygmy shrews – which live in tunnels beneath the hedgerow and feed on beetles, caterpillars, worms and woodlice – are mating now and will produce the first of up to four litters in a month's time. Dormice finally emerge from hibernation this month, though they will go back into a state of dormancy at the drop of a hat if there are food shortages or bad weather. They weave bark and leaves into a summer nest high up in the hedgerow, emerging at night to forage for spring flowers.

Garden and Weather Folklore

The best-known of the May weather sayings is 'ne'er cast a clout till May be out'. A 'clout' was a piece of clothing, so it is obviously a suggestion that you shouldn't remove it, due to the weather being cold, but there is some disagreement about what the rest of the saying means. It could mean until the end of May but it could also refer to 'the may': hawthorn or may blossom. There are about half a million miles of hedgerows in the UK and the vast majority of them contain hawthorn, all of which bursts into white frothy flower in late April and early May. Bring on the may – but don't bring in the may, as it's considered unlucky to bring this blossom indoors.

Beware of the 'ice saints', as they were known throughout northern Europe. They are St Mamertus, St Pancras and St Servatius, whose feast days fall on 11th, 12th and 13th May respectively and who are supposed to bring winter's final blast of cold weather. In France they are the *les saints de glace*. They're known as *ledoví muži*, or ice men, in the Czech Republic, where they are joined by 'cold Sophia' on St Sophia's Day, 15th May. In Poland, they are *zimni ogrodnicy*, the cold gardeners.

'St Urban gives the summer': St Urban's Day on 25th May is one of the (many) days in the year that are said to provide a prediction for the whole of the upcoming period.

In ancient Greece this was the time to eagerly look out for the heliacal rising of the Pleiades, the star cluster also known as the Seven Sisters. Heliacal rising is the moment a star first becomes visible above the eastern horizon pre-dawn, having been lost in the daytime sky, and it happens at roughly the same time annually. For the ancient Greeks, the heliacal rising of the Pleiades in May heralded the beginning of the sailing season, an important date for a maritime society that used celestial navigation.

Garden Wildlife in May

Nights are noisy as this is the key time for mating hedgehogs, known as 'the rut'. Courtship can take hours, as males woo females by circling around, snorting and puffing. If you've ever witnessed this, you will know the females rarely look interested – it's astonishing hedgehogs manage to procreate at all. Not least because all the snorting and puffing attracts rival males who proceed to try their own luck, inevitably ending up in a fight. When mating does happen, it's a delicate affair – the female adopts a special body position with her spines flattened as the male mounts from behind. Contrary to what you might expect from observing this laborious ritual, hedgehogs may have several partners within a season.

The first brood of bumblebee offspring are all 'workers' (sterile females). Some will guard or clean the nest, while others will forage for nectar and pollen from flowers. Some of the nectar will be consumed by these bees, but most will be brought to the nest to feed other workers and the next batch of grubs. From now on, the queen will remain inside the nest, her main job being to lay more eggs.

In the sky, summer migrants – including swifts, swallows and house martins – have arrived from their wintering grounds in Africa, 6,500 kilometres away, and waste no time in preparing to breed. Males arrive a few days before the females to set up territories, and mating begins in earnest with the arrival of the females. By the month's end, every paired summer migrant that arrived earlier in the month will be sitting on a clutch of eggs.

A female bird usually lays one egg a day, at dawn. Clutch size (the number of eggs per nest) depends on the species and food availability. Birds such as tits can have up to 14 eggs per brood. Swifts have three. For most garden birds, only after all the eggs are laid do the birds start brooding them, as this ensures all eggs hatch within a day of each other, so the chicks are easier to feed. Swifts are the exception and have chicks of different ages in the nest at the same time.

The Pond in May

The pond plants are at their lushest and freshest now and are putting on a great burst of growth, quickly threatening to cover the pond. Many are in flower and buzzing with bees. Cuckoo flower, also known as lady's smock, is producing its pale pink flowers, as is water crowfoot – producing its white flowers just above the surface of the water – and the closely related and golden-coloured water buttercup.

Look out for the magical transformation that occurs when a dragonfly nymph hauls itself out of the water. They often choose vertical reeds or the leaves of flag irises, and there the nymph will shed its final exoskeleton, having moulted up to 17 times in the process of growing from egg to adult. At the moment that it climbs out of the top of the exoskeleton, it is the same drab brown as it has been all through its life. It will rest for one to three hours, allowing its body and wings to harden up, and will then take a maiden flight of a few metres. Over the following days and weeks, it will grow stronger, take on its vibrant adult colouring, and become ready to mate.

Tadpoles are beginning to resemble something close to tiny frogs now, while newt eggs are starting to hatch, into larvae rather than tadpoles. They have gills and will live underwater for now, growing into newts over around 90 days. After mating, the older newts leave the pond and head back to the territory they have established on land.

The water now is alive with activity. Dytiscidae beetles dive and hunt among the fern-like spiked water milfoil and the fennel pondweed, while larvae wriggle and dart about just below the surface, and water boatmen skate across the top.

Folk Song of the Month

'The Old Garden Gate'

Traditional, arr. Richard Barnard

A beautiful, sad song about a lover's inconstancy, told on a May morning by the garden gate. This tune was a version collected by Ralph Vaughan Williams in 1903. The lyrics are mainly from an old Wiltshire version collected by Alfred Williams in the early 1900s.

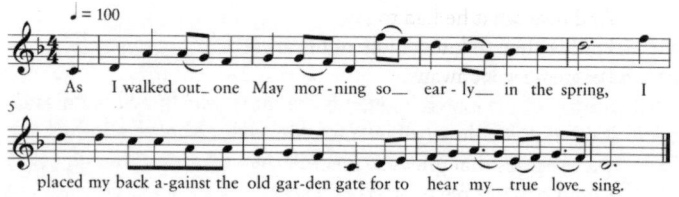

As I walked out one May morning
So early in the spring,
I placed my back against the old garden gate
For to hear my true love sing.

To hear my true love sing a song
And hear what he had to say,
For I wished to know more of his mind
Before he went away.

'Come sit you down all by my side,
On the grass that grows so green.
It's now past three quarters of a year
Since you and I together have been.'

'I will not come and sit down by you
Nor any other man,
Since you have been courting another girl
And your heart is no longer mine.'

I will never believe what an old man says
For his days they can't be long,
And I never believe what the young man says
For they promise but marry none.

There is a flower I've heard them say,
I wish that flower I'd find;
It's called heartsease by night and day
And would ease my troubled mind.

May Dew

Tradition says that if you wash your face in the dew before sunrise on 1st May, you will have a flawless complexion all year. Young women used to stay out all night in woods and meadows on May Day eve to catch it at dawn (though there is some suspicion that this might also have served as an excuse to get up to other things). Dew forms on blades of grass when the air is at 'dew point': saturated until any further cooling will result in water condensing into droplets. In spring the ground is still holding on to the cold of winter, chilling the blades of grass that rise from it, and when the moisture-filled air meets the cold blades of grass, water clings. Autumn is also a dewy time of year, but with the ground still heated after the summer, the dew is more likely to form on objects, such as spider webs strung between branches, that are away from the ground but are chilled by cold night air.

Flower of the Month

Lily of the Valley

Latin name: *Convallaria majalis* (*Convallaria* from
the Latin *convallis*, meaning 'valley', and *majalis*
from the Latin *maius*, meaning 'May').
Common names: May bells, May lily, Our Lady's
tears, Mary's tears, ladder to heaven, mugget (from
the French name for the flower, *muguet*).

Fragrant lily of the valley produces its pure white spikes of bell-like flowers in May. It represents chastity, humility and purity, and as such has traditionally been included in wedding bouquets. In the Victorian language of flowers, it means, 'You've made my life complete'. Aw. There is a French tradition of giving sprigs of lily of the valley to loved ones on 1st May, which is known as *La Fête du Muguet*, Lily of the Valley Day.

How does it appear from the bare ground? Perhaps it sprang from the earth at the foot of the cross when Mary's tears hit the ground, or from the drops of blood shed by St Leonard as he battled the last dragon in England. Or maybe it is just underground rhizomes that sit tight all winter long, waiting for warmer weather. Lily of the valley is almost too easy to grow, becoming invasive, so plant it in a large area where nothing else will thrive. It is gorgeous in pots; and you can buy the rhizomes in winter and pot them up indoors to force these beautifully scented flowers to bloom even earlier in the year.

Inside the Beehive in May

In arable areas, this is boom time, as vast fields of oilseed rape burst into bright yellow flower and the bees go into a frenzy of nectar collection and honey production. Elsewhere, they will visit hawthorn, horse chestnut and other spring blossom and flowers. Forager bees collect nectar until their 'honey stomachs' are full, then return to the hive and pass it to the hive bees (also known as receiver bees), which put it into cells near the top of the frame. Nectar is about 80 per cent water and would quickly ferment, so the hive bees beat their wings furiously to evaporate the water content to below 18 per cent. It is then honey, which will keep indefinitely, and the bees cap it with wax.

If they have space to expand, bees will keep making honey as an insurance policy, even when they have plenty in store. The beekeeper can take advantage of this and add 'supers' – boxes of frames to be filled with honeycomb – above the main brood box. A 'queen excluder' keeps the queen in the brood box and prevents larvae being laid in the supers. Spring honey – usually pale, light and floral, and set if it contains oilseed rape honey – may be harvested towards the end of the month.

Look Out For

Swallows, Swifts and House Martins

By late May, swifts are arriving for the summer from their winter home south of the Sahara, swallows from South Africa, and house martins from equatorial Africa. All have predominantly aerial lifestyles and are beautiful to watch in our skies. They are often confused for each other but are easy to tell apart once you know what to look for. Seen from below, a house martin has an entirely white body, with a black head cap, wings and tail tip; the tail has a shallow crescent scoop. A swallow has a white underbody and marking on each wing, and a red head. Its tail is deeply forked with long, elegant tines. Of the three, swifts are the most often seen over cities and suburbs. The swift's body and wings are brown all over and it has a deep scoop shape to its tail. It emits a distinctive, high-pitched, screeching cry.

A Song for May

'The Feast of Beltane', or *'Samhradh Samhradh'*

Traditional, arr. Richard Barnard

A beautiful song from the early 1600s, traditionally sung in Ireland at Beltane, full of the joys of early summer, with cuckoos calling, fair maidens and golden sun. Although known as 'The Feast of Beltane', *'Samhradh Samhradh'* simply means 'Summer Summer'. The tune is also known as *'Thugamar Féin an Samhradh Linn'*, or 'We Brought the Summer Here Again'.

Samhradh, samhradh, bainne na ngamhna,
Thugamar féin an samhradh linn.
Samhradh buí na nóinín glégeal,
Thugamar féin an samhradh linn.

Bábóg na Bealtaine, maighdean an tSamhraidh,
Suas gach cnoc is síos gach gleann,
Cailíní maiseacha bán-gheala gléasta,
Thugamar féin an samhradh linn.

Repeat chorus

Tá nead ag an ghiorria ar imeall na haille,
Is nead ag an chorr éisc i ngéagaibh an chrann,
Tá'n chuach 's na héanlaith a' seinm le pléisiúr,
Thugamar féin an samhradh linn.

Repeat chorus

ENGLISH VERSION

Summer of summers, milk of the pastures,
We brought the summer here again.
Bright golden sun, the cheerful daisy,
We brought the summer here again.

Beauties of May, the fair maidens of summer,
In every valley, hill and glen.
Girls dressed in white, so lovely and radiant,
We brought the summer here again.

Repeat chorus

The hare has its home up on the high cliff,
The heron's high nest, the song of the wren,
Cuckoos are calling, larks are playing,
We brought the summer here again.

Repeat chorus

June

In the Ancient Meadow

Most meadows peak in June, as colourful and full of life as they are going to be this year. Red and white clovers jostle with anything from field scabious, greater knapweed, ox-eye daisies, salad burnet, bird's foot trefoil and bee and pyramidal orchids. There are hawkbits and vetches, rock roses, thymes and wild marjorams, thistles and fairy flax. The yellow rattle flowers among the grasses. Many grasses are in flower now, too, including the wonderfully named Yorkshire fog, cocksfoot, Timothy grass and creeping bent. Everything drips with pollinators: the red and blue burnet moths, which feed on bird's foot trefoil and pupate in papery parcels on tall grass stems; the myriad of blue butterflies that visit chalk grassland; the speckled woods, which are happier in the shade of a wood meadow; and the ringlets and damp-loving specialists you might find in a wet meadow.

Far north, in the wilds of the Outer Hebrides, the machair lies low to the ground, sheltering itself from the high winds of the Atlantic. *Machair* is a magical Gaelic word that means low-lying, fertile grassland. Here, you'll find the usual meadow wildflowers: clovers, buttercups and lady's bedstraw, but also lesser-known sea rocket, lesser butterfly orchids, common twayblade and sea bindweed. Around the Callanish stones on the Isle of Lewis, bees forage among flowers that have shared the space with stones for some 5,000 years. Here, against the Atlantic winds, grasses fall over themselves and create pockets of shelter for one of our rarest bees, the great yellow bumblebee, which nests among the thatch, protected from the wind by a 'comb-over' of grass. Once widespread all over Britain, these days the great yellow is found only in the outer fringes of Scotland and is widely associated with machair. Without machair there would be no great yellow bumblebees; without great yellow bumblebees, would there be machair?

Kate Bradbury

Garden Craft

Nature Weaving

Weave midsummer flowers and foliage into a piece of nature art. You can do this on any scale you like, from a tiny miniature frame woven with daisies and ivy-leaved toadflax to a huge one featuring whole fern leaves and strips of cordyline.

YOU WILL NEED:
- 3 or 4 sticks to make a frame
- String
- Foliage and flowers
- Feathers
- Ribbons

First make your frame by placing the sticks on the ground and tying the ends together. If you can find a cleft stick you can skip this part as it will provide the framework. Next tie the string to one side and loop it backwards and forwards between two of the opposite sides, until you have lots of lines to weave in between. Tie of string off at the end. Weave your foliage, flowers and feathers through the rows. You can enjoy your woven piece while it is fresh or leave it to dry. The effect will be different but will be beautiful, too.

Inside the Beehive in June

The beehive is reaching full strength now and it may prepare to swarm, particularly if space is running out. This is its way of reproducing itself and creating new colonies. The queen lays eggs in specially prepared queen cells and the resulting larvae will be fed on royal jelly – produced from the heads of the nurse bees – for 16 days. Male drone bees are also raised, their only purpose being to mate with a new queen. On a still, warm day, the old queen will leave the nest (flying for only the second time in her life) with around 60 per cent of the hive – up to 30,000 of her faithful workers all flying in a mass through the June air. The swarm will settle temporarily around a branch of a tree while scout bees search for a new home. Back in the old hive, the new queens fight for dominance, and the victor flies from the nest with a drone bee to mate on the wing, then returns to the hive to take her place as the new queen.

A Jig for June

'Dawns Gwyl Ifan' or St John's Eve Dance

Traditional, arr. Richard Barnard

Throughout Europe, midsummer was traditionally celebrated on St John's Eve and St John's Day, 24th and 25th June, and involved feasting, dancing, singing, fires and flowers. In Wales, St John's Eve and St John's Day are known as *Gwyl Ifan*, and this Welsh jig was traditionally played at *Gwyl Ifan* celebrations.

Later the tune had English words put to it by A P Graves, and as such is called 'Hunting the Hare'. But as that came later, and the words are pretty gruesome, and the tune is such a good one even without them, it is presented here in its original form as a traditional Welsh midsummer dance.

Folk Song of the Month

'The Seeds of Love'

Traditional, arr. Richard Barnard

This is one of the first songs ever collected by celebrated folk-song collector Cecil Sharp. He heard it one morning in 1903, sung softly by gardener John England as he mowed the lawn.

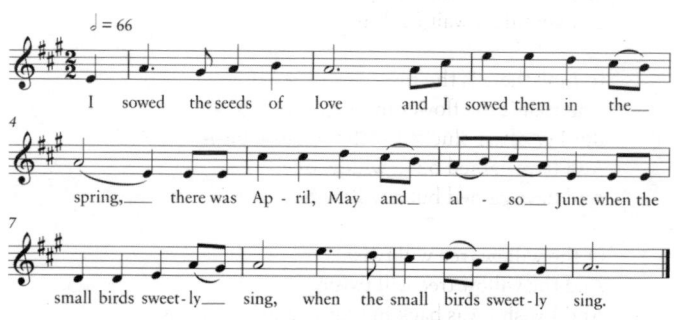

I sowed the seeds of love
And I sowed them in the spring,
There was April, May and also June
When the small birds sweetly sing,
When the small birds sweetly sing.

My garden it was full
With seeds of every kind,
But I had not freedom for to choose
The flower that was on my mind,
O, the flower that was on my mind.

My gardener he stood by,
So I asked him to choose for me
And he chose the violet, lily and the pink,
But I did refuse all three,
But I did refuse all three.

The lily I forsook
Because it fades too soon,
And the pink and violet I did overlook,
So I vowed I'd wait till June,
So I vowed I'd wait till June.

In June there is the rose
And that is the flower for me,
But I've often plucked at the red rose bush
And have gained but a willow tree,
And have gained but a willow tree.

O, the willow tree will twist,
And the willow tree will twine,
And I wish I was back in that young girl's arms
That held this heart of mine,
That held this heart of mine.

Birds of the Month

Dove and Pigeon

The dove is a symbol of Pentecost, which falls in late May or early June. Doves are generally smaller than pigeons but they are in the same family of birds (*Columbidae*), which consists of over 300 species. There are several dove relatives that we can see in our gardens and towns.

The feral pigeon is most probably the bird that many of us see most often, as it has become extremely – often annoyingly – adapted to living on the scraps and mess that humans leave behind. Feral pigeons are descended from escaped domestic pigeons, bred for eating, which in turn are descended from rock doves. Rock doves inhabit sea cliffs and mountain ledges on the northern and western coasts of Scotland, on offshore islands and on the coast of Northern Ireland. Feral pigeons settle wherever they can find crannies that resemble cliff ledges, often the struts under bridges and the nooks of office blocks. They are grey, stout and sturdy, their grey necks overlaid with iridescent pink and green, like an oil slick on a tarmac road.

Collared doves are more delicate: slim, pale and distinguished. They have thin black collars at their necks, and their grey breasts have a blush of pink to them. They often make truly shocking nests, really just a few twigs piled loosely on top of each other with the eggs perched precariously on top. Collared doves are responsible for the soft but relentless 'coo-COOOO-coo' noise that echoes around your house when they perch on top of your chimney.

The turtle dove is an even daintier thing, and sadly far more endangered. It is a bird of Britain's east coast, but is increasingly rare there. You might notice it by its gentle, telephone-like purring coo. It is small, only a little larger than a blackbird, and has a pink-blushed grey breast, black gill-like markings on its neck, and brown and black patterned wings.

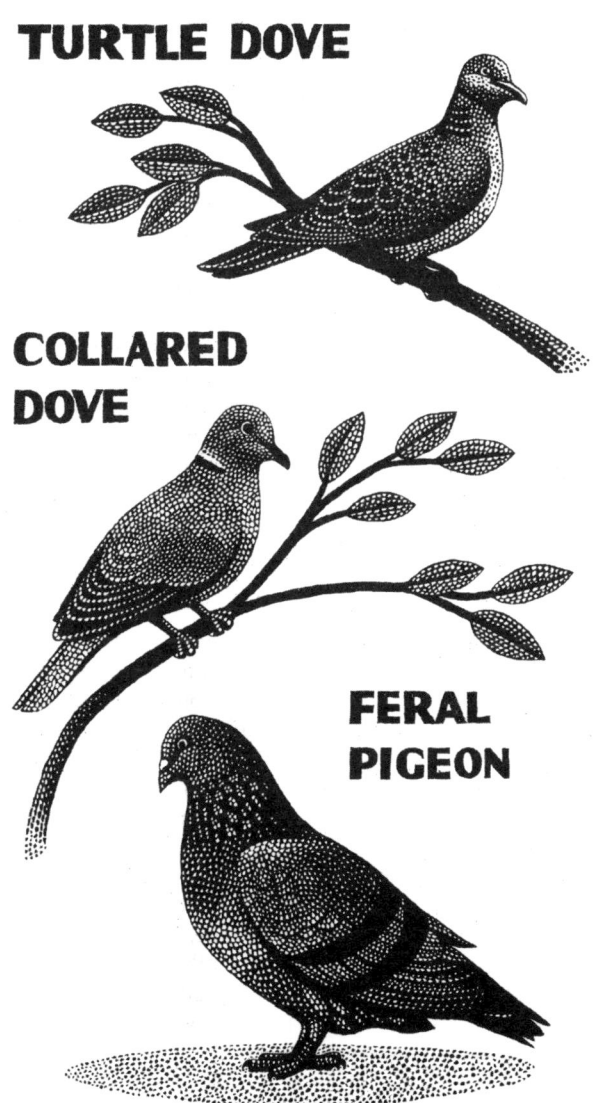

The Hedgerow in June

It is the month of flowers in the hedgerow. All of the hedgerow roses are blooming their hearts out: dog rose and apple-scented sweet briar, as well as the downy rose, the burnet rose and the field rose. They scramble between bramble flowers, white bryony and blossoming honeysuckle up in the heights of the hedge. Between the petals in their elevated nest, the dormouse litter of four or five young has been born. They are pink, furless and blind, and are being carefully looked after by their mother.

Down at the hedgerow base, hoglets – baby hedgehogs – are being born this month and next. They are spineless and blind and the mother nurses them in her dug-out shelter. The badgers are out and about more often, making day nests in the warm weather so that they can sleep above the ground. Cow parsley is still flowering and it has been joined by red campion, common orchids and foxgloves, which seem to be buzzing as bees crawl deep inside the flowers to reach their copious nectar, emerging smothered in pollen. Wild strawberries are ripening, too.

Hummingbird hawk moths and painted lady butterflies are also visiting the flowers. Hawthorn jewel beetles start feasting on hawthorn leaves and laying their eggs there. The larvae will hatch and make zigzag patterns beneath the surface. Small tortoiseshell larvae, having hatched this month on nettles, communally spin a web over themselves so that they can feed in safety.

Midsummer

Another month containing another enchanted time: Midsummer Eve and Midsummer Day. There is only a smattering of such days through the year, but they come thick and fast in early summer. Maybe it's the quality of the light, filtering and pooling through the bright or deep green of midsummer foliage, that encourages fairies. Or perhaps it's the long, languorous evenings, barely turning into true night at all, that have us wanting to stay out late, light fires that spark against the deep blue summer gloaming, and feel the magic of the mid-point of the year.

Midsummer was traditionally celebrated on 24th June, St John's Day – he was the man who foretold Jesus' birth. Unusually among feast days, it celebrates St John the Baptist's birth rather than his death, and it has a particular significance because it falls exactly six months before Jesus' birth. There is always this hint of a mirroring of midwinter at midsummer. We celebrate the joy of light and warmth, knowing that this is the tipping point, when we begin the slow slide towards the cold and dark. Because of this, there is also a strong tradition of attempting to capture the moment and prolong it. Midsummer bonfires were traditionally lit, on beacon hills and in towns and villages, and were kept burning all night. This was one of the few times that long-tended hearth fires would be extinguished, only to be relit using the flame of the midsummer fire. The hearth fires would then be kept burning into the months to come, holding back the coming of winter.

Of course, we can't hold winter back, and we can't capture midsummer – it is as fleeting as all of the other moments of the year. But we can make sure we soak it in. Sit in it, feel the breeze against your skin, and make yourself a picture of your surroundings – how blue the sky is and how warm the air is. Hold this midsummer feeling within you, and tend it like that flame in the hearth, for as long as you can.

July

In the Ancient Meadow

The beginning of the month sees meadows fizz and hum with life: bumblebees coming to the end of their lifecycle for another year, solitary leaf-cutter bees appearing to swim over greater knapweed flowers to collect pollen while scissoring petals from ox-eye daisies to make their cigar-like nests. Some greater knapweeds will be seeding already, and goldfinches will gather to take their seed, ensuring they drop plenty on the ground to provide the knapweed of next year.

Sit still for a while and you will hear the chirrups of grasshoppers and crickets, the click and whirr of chafer beetles, the rustle or 'rattle' of ripe yellow rattle seeds. Delve into the thatch and you may find the elusive caterpillars of meadow brown butterflies chewing at grasses, or hiding until dusk before emerging to feed at night. Look further still, for chrysalises of speckled wood or meadow brown butterflies, for field vole tunnels and for frogs and toads sheltering in the meadow's damp underbelly.

July is also a month of beetles: as the first fists of wild carrot flowers signal a move from mid- to late summer, orange-red soldier beetles descend for weeks of mating. You might spot a longhorn beetle taking shelter in the trumpet of a field bindweed flower, or the iridescent green of a swollen-thighed flower beetle resting on a buttercup. Ladybirds mate vigorously in the hot sun, the females eventually laying eggs on aphid colonies around the flowers of scabious and ox-eye daisies. June is a month of fervent, unrelenting life, and nowhere more so than in an ancient meadow.

Towards the end of the month most flowers will be over, with devil's bit scabious and wild carrot carrying the torch for later pollinators. Seed of yellow rattle will be falling soon, signalling the end of the flowering year, but the beginning of another. Once the rattle has fallen, the meadow is ready to cut, even if some other plants are still in bloom.

Kate Bradbury

The Hedgerow in July

The bramble is still flowering, but the first green fruits are starting to form, and they are joined now by hedge bindweed and the aptly named traveller's joy, the cheerful yellow wild clematis that changes its common name as the year goes on (it will be old man's beard by November). Hedge parsley and wild carrot come into flower this month, both of them resembling cow parsley (though the hedge parsley is a pinker version) and just as attractive to insects who flock to them. All the insects of the hedgerow are busy getting their fill. Speckled wood butterfly, hoverfly, gatekeeper butterfly, Jersey tiger moth, red-tailed bumblebee, seven-spotted ladybird, buff-tailed bumblebee, honeybee, leafcutter bee, ringlet butterfly, painted lady butterfly, green bottle fly, peacock butterfly and small tortoiseshell butterfly might be seen. There are plenty of creatures feasting on the greenery, too, and spotted longhorn beetles are feeding on cow parsley and hawthorn.

July sees the first good crop of fruits, which are a great boon to the residents of the hedgerow. The cherry plums and wild cherries have started to ripen, along with more wild strawberries. Beneath the ground, attached to the roots of hazels, summer truffles have formed and may be dug up by foraging mammals. Hoglets (baby hedgehogs) start to go on foraging trips with their mother. About two weeks later they will set out on their own. Dormouse babies start to forage with their mother when they are a few weeks old. The young creatures' diet has switched from flowers to buds and insects. A common lizard may emerge from the shelter of the hedgerow and take up a position on a well-placed stone to bask in the warmth of the sun.

Inside the Beehive in July

The colony is now at full strength, with thousands of bees setting out all day every day to reap the bounty of the summer flowers. Wild blackberry, clover, rosebay willowherb, poppy, thistle, red campion, meadow cranesbill and gardens full of flowers are all providing nectar for the summer's honey. At the end of June and the beginning of July, lime trees start to flower, providing a major source of nectar, particularly for city bees. This makes a dark amber, complex, slightly minty honey. Some farmers grow borage on a large scale for its seed, and honey from this plant will be very pale and clear. At this time of year the race is on to fill the hive with honey to see it through winter – whatever its look and flavour. Each individual bee will produce approximately one twelfth of a teaspoon of honey in its six-week lifetime, and an average colony will need 25kg of surplus honey to survive to the following spring.

Look Out For

Moths

This is a good time to go moth spotting. At dusk on a warm, dry, calm evening, hang an old white bed sheet over the washing line, shine a lamp onto it from behind, then wait for poplar hawk-moths, cinnabar moths, silver-ground carpets, swallow-tailed moths and others to visit.

Garden and Weather Folklore

The most famous piece of weather lore for July – perhaps even for the whole year – relates to St Swithin's Day:

'St Swithin's Day if thou dost rain, for 40 days it will remain,
St Swithin's Day if thou be fair, for 40 days will rain na mair.'

Although it doesn't hold that one day can foretell 40 more, there is some truth behind this saying. During high summer, our weather tends to lock into a pattern, so whatever that is by the 15th July is likely to continue right up until late August, when autumnal weather begins. Incidentally, rain on St Swithin's blesses the apples and ensures an excellent harvest in autumn.

Some weather lore that has persisted for thousands of years is the idea of the 'dog days'; the hottest, muggiest days of summer, between mid-July and mid-August. The name comes from the heliacal rising of Sirius, the Dog Star, which is the brightest star in the sky. The heliacal rising of a star is the is the moment it first becomes visible pre-dawn above the eastern horizon, having until then been lost in the daytime sky. This happens at roughly the same time annually and is a different phenomenon to the rising of the bright planets (as planets wander across the sky, while the stars are relatively fixed, their timings slipping slowly over time). Sirius's heliacal rising can now be observed in the eastern pre-dawn sky from around 21 August. In ancient Egypt, Sirius's heliacal rising occurred in early July and signalled the Nile would soon flood. In ancient Greece and Rome, it was thought to be a time of bad tempers, bad luck and general unrest due to the stultifying heat. However, in Britain and Ireland it has been seen as a time to wish for dry weather for the harvest:

'Dog days bright and clear indicate a happy year
But when accompanied by rain, for better times our hopes are in vain.'

SEASHELLS

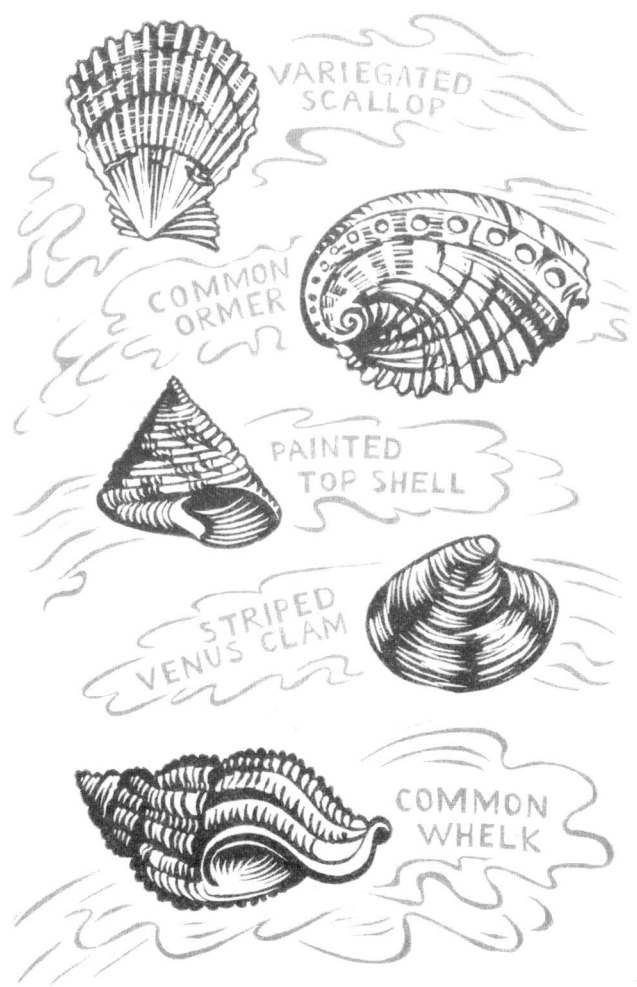

Flower of the Month

Oxeye Daisy

Latin name: *Leucanthemum vulgare* (*Leucanthemum* from the Greek *leukos*, meaning 'white', and *anthemon*, meaning 'flower'; *vulgare* meaning 'common').
Common names: moon penny, moon daisy, dog daisy.

Happy, sunny oxeye daisies once filled the countryside in July, the last hurrah of the hay meadows before they turned their attention to seeding. The old common names of moon penny and moon daisy arose because of the flower's ability to glow in moonlight, and what a sight a daisy-rich meadow must have been on a moonlit July evening. Now, they are most likely to be spotted in hedgerows, which so often act as the final vestiges of the habitats that once surrounded them. Modern agriculture has all but done for the meadows, but oxeye daisies and their companions – valerian, hedge bedstraw, common toadflax and all – cling on at the margins. You may even see diminutive oxeye daisies on cliff edges, in dwarf forms because of the salt-laden wind.

If you wanted to start a meadow of your own, even a small-scale one, the dependable and spectacular oxeye daisy is the place to start – sow the seed in autumn. Alternatively, plant it in a border, where this beautiful wildling will hold its own among the cultivated perennials.

Summer Hailstorms

Hail in summer always feels like a symptom of our crazy, out-of-sync weather but, in fact, hail is naturally a summer phenomenon. The most intense hailstorms occur between May and September, with a defined peak in July. Hail forms in giant cumulonimbus thunderclouds, which grow to great, towering heights in the summer as they are fed by the hot ground creating thermals that lift water vapour high into the air. The tops of these massive clouds are freezing cold, and here drops of water turn to ice crystals. As they start to fall through the cloud, the crystals make contact with other water droplets, which cling to their surfaces. The strong updraughts within a cumulonimbus cloud then whisk thecrystals back up to the top and freeze them again. This circulation can happen numerous times, until the hail pellets grow too heavy and fall to earth.

August

In the Ancient Meadow

A dry late-summer's day is the perfect time to cut the ancient meadow, ensuring the hay is in perfect condition for winter fodder to feed livestock. Traditional cutting methods entailed using a scythe, a tool comprising a long curved blade at the end of a pole attached to one or two short handles. The process often involved teams of farm workers who spent several days cutting the grass in stages, allowing wildlife such as hares and toads to escape to safer habitats (although rabbits and birds' eggs would inevitably have been taken by some labourers for tea). After the cut, the hay was left on the surface to dry out, allowing any flower or grass seeds to fall into the sward beneath. The workers returned to turn it at least once a day to thoroughly dry the crop, which further loosened any remaining seed so it could fall to the ground. Once dry, the hay was loosely piled into haystacks, where most of it lasted into winter. Only the top of the stack would rot, and it would be used in compost the following year.

Later, horse-drawn mowers were used, which sped up the cutting process. These days, industrial mowing equipment clears the space in a day. Machines bale the hay and take it undercover, where it lasts well into winter.

Regardless of cutting method, the cut is best done in stages to maximise biodiversity of flowers and of those who live in the meadow. Some meadow-makers cut around flowering plants so they continue to provide forage for pollinators, while enabling the plants to complete their life cycles by maturing and setting seed. Others provide a year-round 'buffer zone' or margin of long grass, which helps provide long-term shelter for wildlife once the meadow has been cut. Ant hills may also be spared in the cut, enabling ants to continue living in the meadow while also increasing forage for birds.

Kate Bradbury

Garden Craft

Flower and Leaf Mandalas

Mandalas, which involve making beautiful concentric patterns, often with coloured sand, are part of Buddhist and Hindu traditions. They act as a focal point for a moment of calm, and you can use the flowers and leaves in the late summer garden to make one of your own. Choose a still day and make your mandala on the ground, or take flowers and leaves indoors.

You will need:
- Flowers and leaves

Choose one flower for the centre of your mandala. Break open your larger flowers so that you have lots of individual petals to work with. You could put them straight onto the ground or lay large leaves down first, placing them in a circle, on which to position the flowers. Keep on working, adding more rings of flowers and leaves, until you have created a beautiful, colourful and textured piece of temporary nature art.

The Pond in August

As the summer wears on, activity within the pond calms down from the fever pitch of spring and early summer. The water is warm and soupy, algae bloom and duckweed flourishes. The growth around the pond is full and lush and deep green, but tinged with wear here and there. Grasshoppers stridulate from the long, golden grasses surrounding the pond, one of the final mating calls of the year. Swallows and swifts swoop over larger ponds, scooping their last drinks before setting off for Africa. There are more seed heads than there are flowers in the garden, and any ducklings and moorhen chicks have finally left their mothers and set out on their own. Everything is wrapping up now, breeding has taken place, babies have been raised. Minds are turning to winter.

But a few tadpoles may have been left behind. If you see any now, they may have 'Peter Pan syndrome' – that is, they have grown and grown but failed to develop in other ways. This is more likely to happen in a cold summer, and it is nothing to worry about. Tadpoles can overwinter, and if they make it through they will be well set up for next spring, able to grow to maturity ahead of the rest of the pack.

There is still plenty of life under the water's surface. The larvae and nymphs have mostly sunk down into the mud at the bottom of the pond, and there are fewer surface creatures darting about. Predatory larvae of bugs, dragonflies and beetles will still swim up to the top to take drowning flies. Late summer rains will often arrive this month, starting to refill the pond at just the time it should be filled, refreshing both the wildlife and the garden. But before that, the rim of mud surrounding the pond makes it easy to see the footprints of the mammals that have been visiting it, such as voles, hedgehogs and foxes.

Inside the Beehive in August

Come August, there are suddenly fewer flowers, and the foraging is leaner. The height of summer has passed and plants have moved into a new phase: they have been pollinated and their own task is now fruiting and setting seed rather than flowering. The bees continue to work the gardens and hedgerows anyway, to keep nectar and pollen flowing into the hive, albeit far less bountifully than last month. Moorland areas are the exception, as heather starts to flower now, producing a very distinctive honey: dark reddish amber in colour and strong, tangy and woody in flavour. Summer honey is taken this month – the 'supers' (boxes of frames to be filled with honeycomb) are removed, the wax cappings sliced off the honeycomb with a hot knife to reveal the liquid honey within, and the combs spun in an extractor to pull out the golden honey and decant it into jars.

Listen Out For

The Grasshopper Chorus

The sound you can hear as you swish through long late-summer grass, that pulsing 'chik-chik-chik', is grasshoppers doing things their own way. Most mating rituals occurred in spring – with the unarguable logic that the earlier you get your babies born, the stronger they'll be to survive the following winter – but grasshoppers mate in late summer, laying the fertilised eggs into dry ground to hatch next spring. Stridulation, the act of rubbing a row of pegs on their back legs against their forewings, acts as a mating call, and is the sound of late summer.

Migration of the Month

Dragonfly

This month the ponds and lakes of southern England will be visited by quivering and vibrant blue and black dragonflies, hovering and shooting suddenly away, or barrelling headlong through the air, their glassy wings glinting in the sun. These are migrant hawker dragonflies, and they are summer visitors.

Insect migrations are very little understood, partly because it is so hard to track the movements of such tiny creatures. We only really know that dragonflies migrate because several non-native species suddenly appear in summer, including the red-veined darter, the lesser emperor, the vagrant emperor and the migrant hawker, which have been visiting for many years but are now seen in greater numbers. New dragonfly species have colonised Britain in the last 20 years, including the willow emerald damselfly and the small red-eyed damselfly. The dainty damselfly has returned, having last been seen here in 1953. There was a single confirmed sighting of the migrant hawker in the 20th century; four were spotted in southern England in 2006, and then a good number in 2010, particularly in south Essex and north Kent. Numbers are now increasing every year and breeding colonies have been observed in the Thames Estuary and across southern England.

Unfortunately, this increase in numbers is down to climate change. Dragonflies cannot regulate their body temperature and so, as the climate heats up, they need to move to cooler areas in order to survive. There are major shifts in dragonfly ranges across the whole world. It seems likely that as temperatures rise and mainland Europe becomes too hot for many of them in summer, we will see more migrant dragonflies flitting across the English Channel.

Dragonflies can live for up to four years, but most of this time is spent as nymphs, living in water. When they are fully grown and the weather is right, they will climb up a stem and complete their metamorphosis, shedding their skin, pumping up their wings and setting off to look for food and a mate. Once mated, the female will find a calm body of water in which to lay her eggs, and the cycle begins again.

Folk Song of the Month

'Garden Hymn'

Traditional, arr. Richard Barnard

'Garden Hymn' is an old American hymn, in the Sacred Harp choral-singing tradition, which originated in New England and was perpetuated in the American South. Sacred Harp songs are always sung unaccompanied, with four singers each taking a turn in leading. 'Garden Hymn' is thought to have found its way to the British Isles via a visiting preacher around 1804.

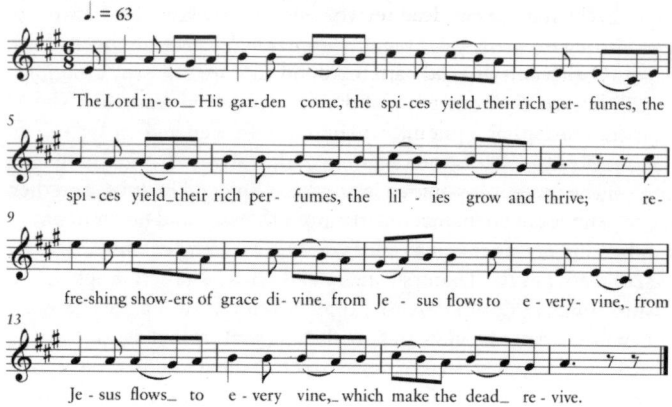

The Lord into His garden come,
The spices yield their rich perfumes,
The spices yield their rich perfumes,
The lilies grow and thrive;
Refreshing showers of grace divine
From Jesus flow to every vine,
From Jesus flow to every vine,
Which make the dead revive.

O, that this dry and barren ground
In springs of water may abound,
In springs of water may abound,
A fruitful soil become;
The desert blossoms as the rose,
While Jesus conquers all His foes,
While Jesus conquers all His foes
And makes His people one.

Garden Craft

Making Leaf Skeletons

Leaves are starting to turn and will soon be falling. Very occasionally, you will find leaf skeletons in the garden: those that have been subject to the exact conditions that allow for the fleshy parts to rot away, and for microorganisms to move in and remove the remnants, but dry and sheltered enough for the skeleton to remain intact. You can recreate these conditions, and create your own leaf skeletons to make into autumnal garlands, turn into cards, or just have as delicate ornaments.

You will need:
- 1 litre water
- 1 tablespoon bicarbonate of soda
- 1 tablespoon baking powder
- A saucepan
- Leaves
- A soft-bristled toothbrush
- Kitchen paper

Put the water, bicarbonate of soda and baking powder into the saucepan and bring to the boil. Drop in the leaves. Simmer for about an hour – topping up with more water if it starts to boil dry – and then remove a leaf to test. The pulp should brush away, leaving the skeleton behind. If it doesn't, return it to the pot for another 15 minutes and try again.

In a shallow tray of cold water, brush the pulp off with the toothbrush. Leave the skeleton to dry on a piece of kitchen paper.

The Hedgerow in August

In the fields alongside the hedgerows, the harvest begins, with great clouds of wheat dust being churned into the air by the combine harvesters. The hedgerow's harvest has begun, too, with berries starting to turn full colour – elderberries, brambles, rowan fruits and haws beginning to ripen. The birds and the little mammals will soon start to eat them and then spread their seed far and wide, so ensuring the next generation of elders and brambles is sown. There are still flowers around, though not so many as in early summer, and they are visited by bumblebees and honeybees, and by red admiral, speckled wood and comma butterflies.

During this warm weather, badgers take some time to dig and extend their setts in preparation for the cooler months, when they will spend more of their time underground. Long-tailed fieldmice are also thinking ahead, building up their larders ready for winter, in a series of tunnels under the hedgerow. They mark the entrances to the tunnels with little piles of stones (which are clearly important, as they will repeatedly replace them if they are moved).

In heat, the slugs that live in the cool, damp base of the hedgerow will go underground, while a snail will plug up the opening in its shell to retain moisture. Hazel boletes, one of the earliest of the year's hedgerow fungi, may be spotted around the roots of hazels.

Offshore Winds, Onshore Winds and Surf

If you are just an occasional bodyboarder or surfer it makes sense to go out during nice, fun, easy waves, and the direction of the wind will have some impact on this. An onshore wind is one that is blowing from the sea in towards the land, and it can make surfing conditions tricky. It makes for messier, choppier waves and encourages waves to break sooner, which can mean that those who want to stay close to the shore miss them completely. An offshore wind – from the land out to sea – cleans up waves and slows wave breaking down, bringing the break closer to the shore and so making waves easier to catch.

Why Are There Two Tides Per Day?

The tides are caused by the gravity of the moon and so you would expect that we would get one tide per day, following the moon around the earth. But no, there are two. The moon and earth are floating in space and orbiting each other, and the moon pulls almost equally on the earth and on the water. But not quite. The water on the side of the earth closest to the moon gets a slightly stronger pull than the earth and so tries to move ahead, towards the moon, causing one of the tides. The water on the side of the earth farthest from the moon gets a slightly weaker pull and tries to lag behind, causing the other. So there are two bulges in the water, giving two high tides per day. The small differences in pull are the result of gravity weakening as the distance from the moon increases.

Bird of the Month

Gull

Of the many gulls that you may see during a trip to the seaside, by far the most likely is the herring gull. It is so ubiquitous that for many of us its cries and calls provide the backdrop to our summer holidays – atmospheric from afar, a proper pain on your chalet roof at 6am. The herring gull is large and confident and can be an aggressive scavenger: watch your pasty if you're eating on the beach. The adult bird has a white head and breast and a grey back and wings with black wing tips. It has a yellow beak and pink legs and feet. In winter it can develop dark streaks on its head.

The black-headed gull is a sociable, noisy bird and, though plentiful on the coasts, it is also the most common inland gull. You are as likely to see it on salt marshes, reservoirs and freshly ploughed farmland as you are at the coast. Despite its name, its head only turns dark in summer and even then it is chocolate brown rather than black. In winter it is almost white all over, except for its black wing tips. Black-headed gulls gather in small flocks and will often roost and feed together in larger groups. This gull's call is said to sound a little like laughter.

Also in the gull family is the kittiwake, which is only really seen at the coast. However, in any cliff colony of seabirds, it is likely to be the most numerous species. Thousands of pairs of kittiwakes balance on their precarious nests made on tiny ledges high above the foaming sea, creating a riot of noise. Unlike many gulls, it does not scrounge on dumps or beaches and instead always feeds at sea. The kittiwake has a rounded head, large black eyes and a small beak compared with other gulls, giving it a much gentler look. Its head and breast are pure white, its back grey and its wing tips black, and it has black legs.

September

In the Ancient Meadow

Wetter meadows often go without a cut, as wet hay doesn't store well. In these circumstances grazing animals such as cows and sheep are brought in this month, to reduce the sward and promote the growth of wildflowers.

On drier meadows, grazing animals are brought back to the land in late summer and early autumn after the hay has been cut. They help to clear up any excess growth left after the cut and prevent the regrowth of grasses, which can outcompete the wildflowers. While they are grazing, the trampling of their hooves pushes seeds into the soil and creates micro-habitats where water can pool and invertebrates such as beetles can set up home.

There is a fine balance between grazing and 'overgrazing', and both the number of grazing animals and the time they are allowed to spend grazing the meadow may be limited.

Now that the grass is cut, molehills become more obvious, especially new ones, as juvenile moles disperse to set up new habitats. Moles both repair and dig new underground tunnels, pushing loose soil, which often contains pieces of chalk, to the surface. The creation of tunnels aids drainage and aerates the soil beneath the meadow, while creating the perfect seedbed for wildflowers on the surface. Larger pieces of chalk may provide a resting habitat for butterflies.

Other disturbance, known as 'rootling', comes from wild boar or pigs, and creates bare patches, uneven ground with troughs and slopes, and areas of exposed chalk, where wildflowers have an advantage over grasses. Along with the wildflowers, species such as spiders, beetles and ants will thrive in these rootled patches, while others, such as skylarks, are thought to use them to find invertebrates to feed their young.

Pigs also eat the roots of competitive plants like creeping thistle and nettles, which compete with more delicate wildflowers. By eating them, the pigs are helping the wildflowers to thrive, greatly improving the diversity of the meadow.

Kate Bradbury

Garden Wildlife in September

As we head into autumn, an old bumblebee queen will lay fewer and fewer eggs, and eventually she and her nest will come to a natural end. Meanwhile, her mated daughters will be feeding on the last of the year's nectar in readiness for hibernation.

Some bees are only just emerging from hibernation, however. The ivy bee is the latest bee on the wing in the UK, flying in the month of September. As their name suggests, these solitary bees feed mostly on ivy flowers, and they nest – often in huge aggregations – in sandy soils, including lawns.

Garden birds are establishing autumn territories this month, with this year's young competing with older birds that are returning to their patch after the summer moult. While most of this takes place fairly amicably, robins and wrens can defend their territories fiercely, and you may spot the odd skirmish.

Some hedgehogs will mate for a second time this month, particularly in the milder south. Food starts to become scarce in autumn, so this can be a huge gamble that doesn't always pay off, as babies emerging from nests in October are rarely able to gain enough weight to see them through hibernation.

As annual plants set seed and die, and perennials and trees shed leaves and store sugar in their roots, there is less available food for soil microbes, which slow down and settle into a quiescent state. Meanwhile, fungal networks start sending up fruiting bodies – mushrooms – this month, which provide food for a range of species, like field mice and beetles, while helping create the next generation of fungi. Most mushrooms exist for just a short time, releasing spores into the wind, before dying back into the soil. These spores survive in a dormant state in winter, ready to inoculate new ground and send out new hyphae (branching filaments) when temperatures increase again.

Charm of the Month

Corn Dolly

The corn spirit lives in the crop, and at harvest time it is made homeless, which can't be good. The idea of the 'spirit of the corn' – corn being a generic name for grain crops such as wheat and barley – was prevalent in pre-Christian, pagan communities throughout Europe. It must have at its heart the vast importance of this crop to the communities that farmed it. Sometimes the corn spirit is male – see the well-known folk song 'John Barleycorn' for a manly personification – but the idea of the 'corn mother' and 'corn maiden' was strong, too.

The harvest would have been carried out by gangs of men, women and children, and the cutting of the final sheaf of corn took on a great significance, representing the end of a period of extremely hard work, the beginning of the harvest feast, and the housing of the spirit of the corn itself. This final sheaf was held up and proclaimed, then taken away and woven or plaited into a dolly that became the centrepiece of the end-of-harvest celebrations. After this, the dolly would be safely housed to keep the spirit of the corn happy over the winter, and in the spring it was ploughed into the earth with the new crop's seeds.

Folk Song of the Month

'The Sprig of Thyme'

Traditional, arr. Richard Barnard

This song, a warning to young women about feckless lovers, plays heavily with the Victorian idea of the language of flowers. There are two possible meanings to the titular 'thyme'. It can just be a play on words, 'let no man steal your thyme/time', but it is also thought to represent virginity, and the rue in the song is associated with bitterness and regret. The song finds us in a garden past its prime and overrun with weeds, looking back at its glory days of summer.

'The Sprig of Thyme' is closely associated with 'The Seeds of Love', our song for June, and often the lyrics and tunes are cross-pollinated. The two are sometimes thought of as variations of the same song from different perspectives. This melody is a version sung by Mrs Jarret in Somerset in 1908.

Come all you pretty fair maids
That are all in your prime,
I would have you weed your garden so clear
And let no man steal your thyme.

For once I had a sprig of thyme,
It prospered by night and day
Till a false young man came a-courting to me
And he stole my thyme away.

O, thyme it is a precious thing,
That grows all under the sun
And thyme will bring all things to an end
And so does my thyme grow on.

But now my garden's overrun
And in it no flowers grew,
For the beds that once had the sweetest of thyme
They are now overrun with rue.

Now it's very well drinking ale
And it's all well drinking wine,
But it's far better sitting by a young man's side
That has gained this heart of mine.

Migration of the Month

Nathusius' Pipistrelle Bat

The first hints that Nathusius' pipistrelle bats were making long autumnal migrations towards the UK and Ireland were when they started turning up on North Sea oil platforms, taking a breather from their mammoth journey, and then hurtling off again into the sea spray. These tiny bats, their bodies just 5–6cm in length, are this month heading our way for a cosy winter hibernation. Central and Eastern Europe, where the bats spend the summer feeding and breeding, have hard, cold winters and so some Nathusius' pipistrelles head south to Spain and Portugal for winter, while others head due west to enjoy the mild and soggy delights that Britain and Ireland can offer.

The bats' spring and summer in Poland, Lithuania and Latvia will have been spent in maternity roosts of up to 350 females, who emerge at dusk and fly through woodland treetops or over bodies of water, eating mosquitos and other flying insects. The males roost nearby and spend hours each night singing social calls to attract females for mating. From the end of July, the babies are born and each female will give birth to and raise a single pup, feeding it with her milk for about four weeks until it is able to fly and set about foraging for itself. By September the offspring are strong enough to join the migration west.

When the bats get here, they will be on the lookout for nooks and crannies such as crevices in cliffs and caves, and tree holes. They make great use of bat boxes. The bats will forage for flying insects, flitting through the treetops at woodland edges and near lakes to build themselves back up after their long flight. They then settle in for hibernation, before emerging and setting off once again across sea and land next spring.

Look Out For

Mushrooms

With autumn rains come autumn mushrooms. These mushrooms are the tip of the fungal iceberg: below the ground the fungus will comprise an often vast network of mycelium, which are strands of fungus that absorb nutrients and moisture from the ground, sustaining it all year round. The fungus exists almost entirely out of sight for most of the year, but autumn rains signal that it is time to fruit and to spread its spores. The mushroom we see is the fruiting body, which will emit microscopic spores that can spread on the wind, alight elsewhere and create new fungal life.

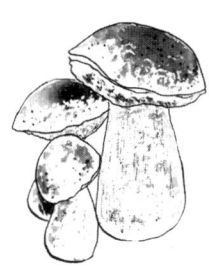

Autumn Equinox

Thre autumn equinox is associated with the harvest, and some harvest traditions take their timing from it. The Harvest Moon is the full moon nearest to the equinox, and Harvest Home or Ingathering, the day of end-of-harvest celebrations, was traditionally celebrated on the Sunday nearest the Harvest Moon.

This is because the autumn equinox is the moment we must start to say goodbye to summer, reap its rewards and prepare for winter. The earth is back at the point now where its tilt is side-on to the sun, just as it was at the vernal/spring equinox in March. This means that – momentarily – no hemisphere is favoured. Day and night are roughly even, all over the world, and the moment of the equinox occurs when the sun is directly overhead at the equator. But this time, the sun will slip a little further south, rather than north as it did in March. From then on, those of us in the northern hemisphere will have a slightly longer night than day, and this will continue until the winter solstice in December. For the southern hemisphere, this is, of course, the spring equinox, and the days will become longer and lighter now.

Nature Table

Mark the Autumn Equinox

- Make an autumn altar: a bowl of produce from the garden, a bunch of late-summer flowers in a jar, rosehips and acorns, orange candles.
- Plant tree seeds in pots of garden soil and keep them outside. Many tree seeds need a winter of cold before they will germinate. Look forward to the spring equinox, when you will hopefully see the first shoots.
- Fill a spray bottle with water, 1 teaspoon of vodka and 25–30 drops of autumnal essential oils, then shake it up and spritz it around. Try: cinnamon, cedarwood, cardamom or ginger.

SMALL MAMMALS

The Hedgerow in September

This is the second great harvest month in the hedgerow year. The hedgerow is dripping with abundant fruits turning fat and shiny, and the hazelnuts are maturing and dropping to the ground. Even the honeysuckle has switched from flowering to berrying. The bramble harvest is in its final throes, and the leaves start to take on shades of autumn, as do the leaves on the rowan trees. Crab apples start to fall. The small mammals – wood mouse, bank vole, hedgehog, common shrew and hazel dormouse – scurry about laying food aside for the winter or feeding themselves up for a long sleep. Fiery milkcap mushrooms may appear near the roots of hazels.

There are increasingly fewer butterflies around, though you may see small tortoiseshells and red admirals. Some caterpillars start to form chrysalises in which to overwinter around now, while most others prepare to overwinter as caterpillars. Wasps, which have been feeding on aphids all summer and being rewarded by their queen with sweet treats, are kicked out of their nests around now, and so they hungrily seek out sweetness in hedgerow berries and fallen crab apples. On warm autumn mornings, tiny money spiders climb to the top of the hedgerow, spin a line and let it catch the gentle breeze, then lift off to fresh territories.

Inside the Beehive in September

In September, the colony shrinks in size as the female worker bees reach the ends of their natural lives and are not replaced in such great numbers. The male drones are no longer needed and would use up precious winter supplies, so they are harshly ousted from the hive and left to die. Natural sources of food for the bees become scarce, but gardens planted with late summer flowers step into the gap, as does Himalayan balsam. This is an invasive and ecologically damaging plant in waterways, but offers a good source of late nectar. Wasps can become pests as they are ousted from their own nests and seek the sweet rewards they have been used to receiving from their own queen, so they may attack hives for honey. The bees shore up gaps in the hive and reduce the size of the entrance with propolis (a resin collected by the bees from tree buds, mixed with beeswax and their saliva).

Look Out For

Daddy Longlegs

Here they come every September, lolloping drunkenly along and bashing off of windows, ceilings and – uh! – faces. This is the month of the daddy longlegs, more correctly called crane flies. The larvae (known as leatherjackets) have spent the summer below grass, munching on roots and decaying plant matter. When autumn rains loosen the soil and signal that it is time to hatch, the daddy longlegs rise haphazardly into the air. They will live for a maximum of two weeks, mating and laying, and providing a rich source of food for birds heading into winter.

October

In the Ancient Meadow

You'd be forgiven for thinking the meadow is on pause between now and spring. Grazing animals may be brought to the meadow periodically to feed, but otherwise it appears quiet, the stumps of grasses and shorn wildflowers the only hint of summer past. But look closer and you will see life.

On mild days, flowers might bloom, including dandelions and rogue relics of summer: viper's bugloss, oxeye daisy and greater knapweed. Despite the lateness of the year, the yellow dung fly is still active: males gather around the dung of grazing cows, horses and sheep, waiting for females, who they can mate with before the females lay eggs. The larvae burrow into the dung and feed on the larvae of other flies living in it.

Some dung beetles may also still be active. They take the dung and tunnel down into the soil with it, burying it and recycling its nutrients into the earth, while also breaking up the ground and improving drainage.

In mild conditions, earthworms will also be active, and you may see gulls dancing on the meadow to trick worms up to the surface, so they may eat them.

Flocks of meadow pipits hunker down in the thatch, feeding on the remains of invertebrates and the odd seed left from the autumn cut. Any disturbance will see them suddenly fly up and off to somewhere more quiet, with a typically jerky flight.

A fox may slink across the landscape, or a hare might venture out to feed on tussocks of grass. By night, hedgehogs may snuffle onto the meadow to feast on the last of the year's beetles, while badgers may be on the hunt for earthworms. On mild days, caterpillars may nibble on leaves – there's always life, if you look for it.

Kate Bradbury

Garden Craft

Make Halloween Nature Wands

Two methods are included here for making a Halloween nature wand. The first produces a beautiful 'jewelled' wand, while the second is a quick and easy wand a child can make while simultaneously enjoying a nature walk or a Halloween party.

FOR A 'JEWELLED' WAND, YOU WILL NEED:
- A stick about 30cm long
- Coloured threads, such as wool or embroidery thread offcuts
- Feathers, leaves, seed heads and beads

Tie a thread around one end of the stick and use it to secure a special feather or pair of colourful leaves, then continue winding it around the stick to create a band of colour. Work down the stick in this way, using different coloured threads and different found objects, interspersed with beads.

FOR A MAKE-AS-YOU-GO WAND, YOU WILL NEED:
- A stick about 30cm long
- Double-sided sticky tape or masking tape
- Tray of autumnal nature finds (optional)

Wind double-sided sticky tape around the stick, or do the same with masking tape with the sticky side facing outwards. The child can now take their wand on a nature walk and collect items by sticking them to the wand as they go. Or for a Halloween party activity, give children a tray of objects that you have gathered yourself.

Preparing for Hibernation

The mists really do start to roll in with the beginning of this beautiful month. They are the result of the ground chilling overnight as nights lengthen and the northern hemisphere tips further away from the sun. The leaves are turning brilliant shades of red and gold, and everything is ripening and closing down for the cold months ahead.

This is the month that we really start to feel the coming winter, nudged along rather rudely by the hour change at the end of the month. We can be clinging to the last vestiges of hope that winter won't be too bad, that the nights are perhaps not as long and cold as we have remembered, and then...bump. The hour changes and our day is cut short, our commute plunged into darkness.

It is hard not to resent this in the moment that it happens, and in the following days as we wrestle with this new dose of darkness just when we need it least. We always want the last dregs of summer to carry on. But try not to fight it. The dark and cold are here for a good reason. Look around you and you will see that everything in the natural world is closing down – you can take the darkness as a cue to do a little of this yourself. We need rest times as well as active times in order to stop ourselves from burning out. This moment is as strong a signal to rest as you are ever going to receive, just as it is to the plants, the mammals and the insects. They know what to do, but we need to teach ourselves. A suggestion: treat yourself to some new pjs if possible, get into them as soon as you get home in the evening, perhaps after a hot scented bath, and then snuggle on the sofa with candles and crumble, and feel your shoulders dropping. Repeat.

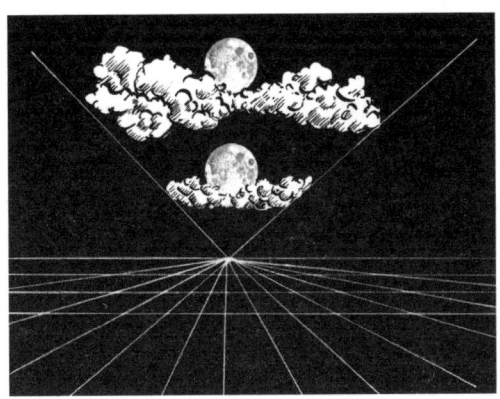

The Moon Illusion

The Harvest Moon, the full moon closest to the autumn equinox, is one of the most remarked-upon full moons of the year, noted for being huge and orange. It can fall in either late September or early October. The colour is related to the harvest: crop harvesting throws lots of dust up into the atmosphere, which scatters green, blue and purple light waves so that we are left looking at the red, orange and yellow, particularly when the moon is low.

The apparent size is down to the 'moon illusion', whereby the moon always looks larger when it is closer to the horizon. In fact, it is always roughly the same size, but landscape features like trees, mountains and buildings appear smaller the farther away they are. When the moon is close to the horizon, we directly compare the visual sizes of distant objects with the visual size of the moon. A distant tree might be completely silhouetted by the moon, making the moon appear huge. We cannot do this when the moon is high in the sky. Added to this can be the timing of this particular moon. The full moon always rises just after the sun sets. Through summer, this has been pretty late in the evening but, once we are past the equinox, it is suddenly much earlier. We might be more likely to be out and about and so more likely to spot it actually rising above the horizon, looking its largest and most golden.

The Pond in October

Falling leaves are drifting onto the surface of the pond now, and the growth around the edges is dying back, taking on shades of gold, brown and red. The reeds and rushes are bowed from rain and wind, and spiders' webs are strung between them. The pond is filling up again with autumn rains and could be brimful by the end of the month.

This month, frogs will go into their version of hibernation, called brumation, a period of dormancy in which they will shut down their bodies to preserve energy. A frog absorbs oxygen in three different ways: through the lungs, as you might expect; through the lining of the mouth; and via the skin, which must be moist at all times. Some will actually hibernate at the bottom of the pond, digging into the mud and sitting out the coldest weather. Others will create their hibernaculas (winter quarters) in the mud at the edge of the pond. Still others, including the year's juveniles, will find nooks and crannies in log or rock piles nearby – anywhere they can stay moist and keep off the worst of the cold until spring. You might spot a particularly fat frog at this time of year. This will be a female, already full of spawn, which she will carry all through the winter, ready for breeding time next February or March. Toads overwinter in old upturned flowerpots, in piles of leaf litter or under large stones.

The first frosts are a signal to many that the time for preparation is past, and the moment has come to tuck themselves away. Everything either dies with the coming of the frosts or takes to the nooks and crannies around the pond. The surface, once alive with pond skaters and whirligig beetles, is still and quiet. The pace of life has slowed dramatically, and the pond is ready for winter.

Great reedmace

Greater pond sedge

Soft rush

The Hedgerow in October

All of the hedgerow leaves are now colouring or falling. Shades of red, yellow, brown and even tinges of purple cling on between the late hedgerow harvest of rosehips, elderberries, sloes and haws. Spiders are at their largest and most mature, with many of them pregnant, too. They are highly visible on webs strung extravagantly across the hedgerow, as if this is their time. The webs catch the dew from the night mists that begin about now, and the droplets may even freeze like beautiful strings of jewels as the first frosts of the year hit.

The hazel dormouse is busy building a new nest especially for winter, at ground level and sheltered by dead wood, moss and leaf litter. Dormice will then go into their long and deep hibernation until next May. Hedgehogs will also go into hibernation this month or next, and need to eat as much as they can to build themselves up ahead of this. Badgers do not hibernate but are feeding on fallen crab apples, brambles and acorns to put on fat reserves ahead of winter.

With autumn rains, the mosses on dead branches and at the base of the hedgerow start to produce and release their spores – their equivalent of seed – which will be carried through the air to land and germinate on moist soil and create new mosses. Rains also encourage mushrooms and other fungal fruiting bodies to appear: chicken of the woods, beefsteak fungi, ethereal, pure white porcelain fungi on dead beech, bracket fungi on spindle and oak; and many more.

Garden and Weather Folklore

If there is a period of warm weather towards the end of October, it is called St Luke's Little Summer. It is said to start around St Luke's Day, on the 18th, and be brought to an abrupt close by St Simon and St Jude, who share the 28th as their feast day. Simon and Jude also pop up as summer busters in a rhyme about Michaelmas daisies, which are always in flower on Michaelmas Day, 29th September.

'The Michaelmas Daisies, among dead weeds, bloom for
  St Michael's valorous deeds.
And seems the last of flowers that stood, till the feast of
  St Simon and St Jude.'

However the two saints don't always bring things to a halt. There is also the possibility of All Hallows Summer, which is unseasonably warm weather around All Hallows Eve (Halloween) on the 31st. In Greece, there is the Little Summer of St Demetrios, which sometimes spans the last two weeks of the month and is a final burst of good weather, allowing sheep to be led to winter grazing fields.

Old Michaelmas Day falls on 10th October (or some say 11th October), a result of the calendar reform of 1752 when 11 days were lost. This is the day on which Michael threw the Devil out of heaven. Having landed on a blackberry bush, the Devil cursed it, spat on it or worse. It is not a good idea to pick and eat blackberries after this date.

NATIVE TREES – SEEDS

Flower of the Month

Marigold

Latin name: *Calendula officinalis* (*Calendula* from the Latin *kalendae*, meaning 'calendar' or 'first day of the month', either from the plant's efficacy in treating menstrual disorders or from the fact that they bloom most months of the year; *officinalis* indicates medicinal properties and uses).
Common names: pot marigold, ruddles, Scotch marigold, marybud, holligold.

The name marigold comes from Mary's gold, as they are in vibrant flower during the Feast of the Annunciation of Mary on 25th March. Clearly, March is at the other end of the year, but as the Latin name *Calendula* points out, marigolds flower all year round, and they are certainly blooming now in their Hallowe'en-friendly shades of pumpkin and fallen leaf. Another plant that goes by the name is the Aztec marigold, *Tagetes erecta*, which is strongly associated with the Mexican Day of the Dead, *Día de Muertos* (which itself has connections to Hallowe'en). They are used as glowing orange grave decorations, to attract the souls of the dead. Calendulas themselves have links to witchcraft, weather divining and medicine. Hung over a doorway, they ward off evil, and if a marigold hasn't opened by 7am, there will be a thunderstorm. Marigolds' medicinal uses are many: to treat stomach ulcers, menstrual cramps, dermatitis, skin inflammations, burns and more. They are edible, too – sprinkle some petals over your Hallowe'en pumpkin soup.

These annuals should be sown in spring, or in autumn for early flowers next year. They are great self-seeders, so once might be enough.

First Frosts

First frosts are coming, tuck up your tender plants. Indeed for a few in the Highlands of Scotland they could have already hit. Next in line is central Scotland, where first frosts often arrive between the end of September and the first two weeks of October. The English Midlands, central Ireland and Dublin are next, around the last week of October. They are followed by the rest of inland England and Wales and the coasts of Scotland and western Ireland in the first week or so of November. The east coast of England starts to get frosts around mid- to late November, with the south and west coasts of England and the Gulf Stream-favoured parts of the west coast of Scotland and western Ireland as late as early December. The Scillies and the Channel Islands often get away scot-free. Take this guide with a pinch of driveway salt: first frost dates vary greatly year by year, so use it as a guide to getting ahead, not a chance to procrastinate.

Inside the Beehive in October

Just as all sources of nectar for the bees are drying up, ivy comes to the rescue by flowering copiously in October. It is covered in bees and wasps seeking out the last of summer's sweetness and sustenance. A hive near ivy may find enough food to spur the queen into laying a final brood of eggs to be raised by the colony; these new young winter bees will live for six months and carry the colony into next spring. The beekeeper will 'heft' the hive around now to see if it contains enough honey to see the hive through winter. The bees will have the honey in the brood box to overwinter on and the beekeeper may leave one or two 'supers' (boxes of frames) full of honey as well. However, some beekeepers prefer to keep all the bees in a smaller area to help them stay warm through the cold winter nights, and to top up through winter with sugar water should the honey run low.

November

In the Ancient Meadow

The ancient meadow seems quiet in November, but stay awhile and you are sure to see a variety of birds. Blackbirds, robins and song thrushes may hop over the sward, feasting on small snails, hibernating caterpillars, spiders and other grubs; the blackbird turning over fallen leaves to see what's sheltering beneath them. Blackbirds and robins have larger-than-average eyes for their size, which helps them see better in the dark. On mild mornings, usually before or around dawn, you may catch them pulling earthworms out of the ground. Any small pools of water will serve as a drinking or bathing station, while grazing-animals' excrement will attract flies and beetles, providing a welcome source of food as the day length decreases.

As well as our native species, look out for migrant birds that arrive, sometimes en masse, in autumn. Redwings and fieldfares come from Scandinavia, and roam the countryside in large mixed flocks, looking for food. They eat insects and other invertebrates, such as worms, but also berries and fallen fruit from nearby hedgerows. In a wood meadow, where flowers and grasses grow beneath trees, redwings and fieldfares find food in abundance, as there may be food to eat from the meadow as well as fruit from the trees.

Look out, also, for winter geese such as pink-footed, barnacle and dark-bellied brent, which gather in huge, honking flocks in wet meadows, eating any remaining plant material and sheltering invertebrates. They may be joined by lapwings, which wheel around winter skies, coming to ground to feed on earthworms. Often lapwings roost by day and feed at night, so you may spot them sleeping.

Some winter birds gather in the same spot each year, such is the abundance of a particular type of food. For them, the ancient meadow provides a place to gather safely in the daytime, providing morsels of food that offer a lifeline during the harshest time of the year.

Kate Bradbury

Nature Table

Making a Space for November

The cusp of October and November brings with it many traditions that serve as invitations to mourn and to remember those that we have lost, and this can provide a beautiful way of using a November nature table, echoing European All Souls' Day traditions on the 1st and Mexico's *Día de Muertos* (Day of the Dead) on the 2nd. Samhain, which straddles October and November, is thought to have been a festival to mark the beginning of winter and to honour ancestors. Fill your table with photographs of your own ancestors, mementos of them and scraps of poetry. Surround them with chrysanthemums, the flowers traditionally used in France to decorate graves on All Souls' Day, and with your seasonal finds.

YOUR TABLE THIS MONTH MIGHT INCLUDE:
- Autumn leaves
- A bowl of chestnuts
- Chrysanthemums in oranges, yellows and reds
- Orange or white candles
- Pictures of loved ones who have died
- Bare twigs
- Mushrooms
- Pumpkins
- Apples

Light your candles and think about those that you have lost, maybe taking a moment to write down a few thoughts that you can tuck into the nature table. Think too about the countryside at the moment, how everything is closing down and dying, but that light and life and spring will come around again.

Garden and Weather Folklore

Samhain on the 1st November was long considered the beginning of winter, after a great feast thrown on the 31st October to say a final farewell to any remnants of summer. Just as at the beginning of the year, there are a couple of pieces of weather lore that suggest that whatever the weather is now, it will not last:

'Ice in November to bear a duck,
Nothing after but mud and muck.'
'On the first of November if weather hold clear,
An end to what sowing you do to this year.'

Despite the cold and dark there is still the possibility of an Indian summer, a term that is often used for any spell of mild and sunny autumnal weather but which specifically means a warm spell on the nine days between Martinmas, on the 11th November, and the 20th November. It is characterised by sunny, hazy days and is also known as Martinmas summer.

It is traditionally said that Martinmas holds particular sway in setting the direction of the wind, and therefore the severity of the rest of winter. 'If the wind is southeast on Martinmas, it will stay there till Candlemas' and so will make for a mild winter. On the other hand, if it is a north wind, this suggests a hard winter to come.

St Catherine's Day, the 25th, was the day to look further ahead:

'At St Catherine's, foul or fair,
So it will be next Februair.'

And finally, St Andrew's Day, on the 30th November, was known in Sweden as *Andersdagen* or *Anders* and was traditionally used to forecast the weather for Christmas Day. '*Anders slaskar, julen braskar*', means 'slushy St Andrew's Day, frozen Christmas'.

Garden Craft

Preserving Leaves

Beautiful autumn leaves gradually fade and lose their colour over time. This is a way to preserve them, then you can string them together into garlands, create falling-leaf mobiles, or use them to make pictures or cards. There are two methods of preserving: one for single leaves and the other for whole stems.

For single leaves you will need:
- Colourful single leaves
- A shallow tray or vase
- Glycerine (from pharmacies and many supermarkets)
- Pebbles
- Kitchen paper

Place the leaves in the shallow container and make up a mixture of one part glycerine to two parts water – just enough to cover the leaves. Use pebbles to weigh down the leaves. Leave to soak for five days, then remove and pat dry with kitchen paper.

For a whole stem/branch you will need:
- A stem or branch of autumn leaves
- A bucket of warm water
- Glycerine
- A vase
- A hammer

First, immerse the stem into a bucket of warm water for about two hours. Mix up a solution of one part glycerine to two parts water in a vase, filling it to at least halfway. Recut the stem and then use the hammer to bash the base of the stem until it is mashed and broken apart, to allow for greater absorption of the glycerine. Place the branch in the vase out of direct sunlight. Beads of glycerine solution will appear on the tips of the leaves when they have soaked up all they can, after about five days. Remove the branch from the solution and hang it upside down to dry.

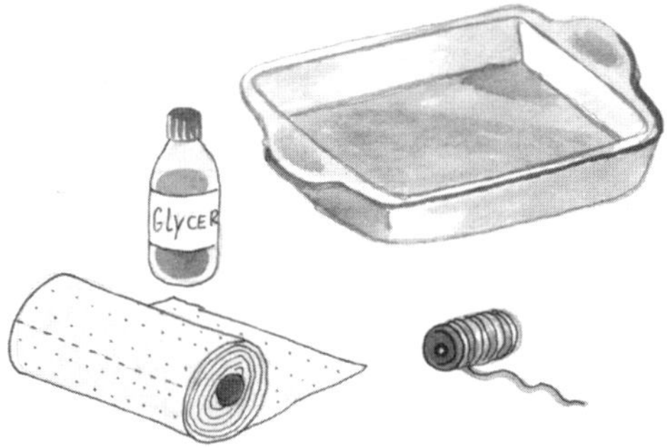

Garden Wildlife in November

On sunny and mild days, it can appear as though autumn hasn't arrived yet. Dragonflies and butterflies may still be on the wing, while the last of the year's hoverflies and wasps will be feasting on the dregs of the ivy flowers. Yet all of these species will have hibernacula (shelters in which to overwinter) to go to and, as temperatures drop, they will disappear.

In their pre-made hibernacula, lined with dry leaves and moss, hedgehogs settle down and their body temperature drops to match their surroundings, so they enter a state of torpor. They need to weigh around 600g to have enough fat reserves to survive hibernation. Those that don't – including last month's 'autumn orphans' – will continue feeding throughout winter. This can be a dangerous time as food is in short supply, so you can help by leaving out cat biscuits for them. If you see a hedgehog out during the day, call your local rescue centre for advice, as it will almost certainly need taking in.

While most species are tucked up and asleep, garden birds are awake, seeing out the few hours of daylight each day. This is a difficult time for birds, as low temperatures and short days mean they need more food but have less time to find it. When it's cold, birds fluff up their feathers to trap heat, as well as shivering to keep warm. With their high metabolic rate, they can burn a lot of calories doing this. They scour branch tips, buds and the skeletal remains of plants to seek out overwintering insects, and they turn leaves on the ground to search for morsels sheltering beneath them. Seeds, berries and rosehips are important sources of winter food, and we can help by not cutting back plants or tidying away leaves in our gardens. Filling feeders with seeds and suet balls can also help to give birds the calories they need, although natural food is always best. We must keep feeders clean to prevent the spread of diseases like avian pox and trichomonosis.

Migration of the Month

The Atlantic Run

Up Scottish rivers such as the Spey, the Tay, the Dee and the Tweed, as well as the Tyne in northeast England, come the silvery Atlantic salmon this month and next, as they return to the gravel beds of their birth. The time (up to four years) they've spent in the oceanic feeding grounds north of the Arctic Circle has meant they are in tiptop condition for the journey. As they arrive in the estuaries, they are met by fresh water, which immediately alters their bodies: they switch from using their longitudinal red muscles, which are useful for long-distance ocean swimming, to using their diagonally oriented white muscles, for thrashing from side to side. This gives them the power to leap up waterfalls and push against the current. They also darken in colour and the males develop strong jaws for fighting off other males when they reach the spawning grounds.

The salmon's homing instinct is uncanny, and the majority will return to the exact stream of their birth. They have an incredible sense of smell and it is thought that each stream and river has its own scent, which the salmon follow, catching a whiff of it in the estuaries and following it upstream.

Once they arrive at the spawning grounds, a female will select a 'riffle', an area of shallow water that flows fast and relatively turbulently over the gravel. She uses her tail to create a shallow depression, called a 'redd', where the eggs can nestle out of the current, and lays up to five thousand eggs into it. A male approaches and deposits his sperm into the redd, and the female covers the fertilised eggs by disturbing the gravel on the upstream edge of the redd. She then moves further upstream and creates another redd. This process is repeated up to seven times until all of her eggs are used up.

Spawned salmon only rarely return to the sea. The longer they are out of sea water, the more they deteriorate, and they nearly always die soon after spawning. The eggs will hatch after a few months and the small fish will live and feed in the river for up to three years before making their journey out to sea.

The Pond in November

The leaves are falling fast now as the temperature and light levels drop. The water of the pond is starting to cool dramatically, and to survive this, the pond and the creatures in and around it are pretty close to being completely dormant. This is where the preparations you have made for wildlife in the garden really come into their own. All summer long the creatures of the pond and the garden have been happily living their lives, feeding and breeding, but now the edges of the garden become their refuge from the cold, and the messier you have left them, the better. It is not only amphibians and mammals that make use of these nooks and crannies. Pond skaters and other aquatic invertebrates overwinter, and will often cluster themselves into a nook in a woodpile.

Leaf piles, compost heaps and upturned broken pots all have their parts to play. If you have not put any into place, it isn't too late to knock some together now. A great number of creatures also see out the winter in the muddy bottom of the pond, popping up to the surface every now and then to take a breath of air, and then sinking back into the depths. The frogs that have hunkered down at the bottom will move around on sunny and warm days. Look out for one swimming across the bottom when the weather is mild, or popping up to the surface for a breath of air.

Foxes, which do not hibernate, make use of the pond now, making night-time visits to its edges to take a drink. You may notice their footprints in the mornings in the mud surrounding the pond. You may also see the footprints of blackbirds around the pond edges, where they will pick through the mud and plants searching for grubs and insects.

Grey heron

Urban fox

Hedgehog

Grey squirrel

Bird of the Month

Starling

This is the month to see starlings in all their glory. A murmuration (from a medieval Latin word meaning 'murmuring' or 'grumbling') of starlings is one of the wonders of the natural world. These masses of swooping and swirling birds that blacken the sky start appearing this month. During the winter, starlings have daytime roosts in high perches where they can see all around for predators, but at night they gather in huge numbers to roost in areas with plentiful supplies of food. Before they settle for the night, they set off in their great swooping clouds, moving almost as one, like a shoal of fish, creating huge columns, swirls and twists in the sky. Scientists have discovered that each bird in the murmuration tracks the seven birds closest to it and copies their movements, and this is why we see a sort of ripple of movement through them.

Starlings on their own are far less majestic. Dark and speckled all over, they are a little smaller than blackbirds and are a bit scruffy-looking. They make a variety of sounds that, on the whole, are not particularly musical and are a little on the screechy side, but that also include buzzes and trills and mimicry of other birds and of the sounds around them. If you can't get out to a wetland or reserve to see the murmurations, you may well see starlings in smaller gangs on your lawn, which they will probe in search of earthworms.

In spring, the male builds a basic nest and then puffs himself up and sings to attract a mate. When she comes near, he waves his wings, fans his tail and hunches his back. Hopefully entranced, she will then complete the nest. By some unknown mechanism and for some inexplicable reason, if there are several pairs of starlings nesting within an area, these community-minded birds will synchronise their laying, perhaps increasing the chances of success for the collective.

The Hedgerow in November

As the hedgerow turns increasingly brown and bare, there are still flashes of colour to be found. Chief among these are the rosehips, the shiny postbox red of the dog rose and the dark purple of burnet rose, but the bizarre fuchsia-and-orange spindle fruits give them a run for their money, looking like an art-teacher's earrings. Hawthorn leaves turn shades of purple in the cold and their haws a deep red, while guelder rose leaves turn pinky yellow, all the better to make their remaining red fruits stand out. There are strings of bright-red woody nightshade berries against bare stems and browning foliage. The fruits of the wayfaring tree are turning from red to black, and the dusty purple sloes are ripe on their bare stems, at their sweetest now after they have been touched by the first frosts. Above all of this hang the fluffy seed heads of wild clematis – old man's beard – looking like strings of fairy lights if they catch the low winter light. The male fern and the soft shield fern have died down, leaving just the evergreen hart's-tongue fern to plod on through winter. Wood blewits have come into season, and beautiful and weird scarlet elf cup fungi appear on dead and decaying wood, as do shaggy parasol mushrooms. The berries on spikes of lords-and-ladies are turning lipstick red. Amid all this ripening and dying down, one plant bucks the trend: ivy starts flowering about now and is visited by grateful wasps, bees and green lacewings that are after the sustaining sips of nectar.

Down at the base of the hedgerow, mammal activity is minimal as the small animals snuggle in burrows or nests against the cold. Deer make use of the hedgerow for shelter from winds and storms.

SEEDHEADS OF THE HEDGEROW

Inside the Beehive in November

All bee activity is starting to close down as the nights lengthen, the weather cools, and the bees rarely leave the hive. They must fill their stomachs with honey from their stored supplies in order to keep their body temperature up, and any foray outside will require more fuel. It is better to sit tight. Bees will naturally die through the winter, and as colonies get smaller they can be at great risk from harsh conditions. But strong colonies containing plenty of bees and a young queen can withstand a very harsh winter. They may even raise a small brood when the weather is mild, though mostly the queen will take a rest now and conserve her own energy. The beekeeper will fit a mouse excluder over the entrance – a piece of metal with bee-sized holes – as mice like to enter beehives in winter and nest there for the ready supply of food.

Look Out For

Rookeries

As leaves fall from trees, rookeries become easier to spot. Rooks make bulky, twiggy nests high up in trees and have a habit of gathering together, often in built-up areas. They also make a lot of noise, with their cry a harsh and raucous 'kaah!'. All of this, combined with their Gothic looks, makes people find their presence disturbing, but they are actually highly intelligent and sociable birds.

Mellow Mists

With the lengthening of nights come mists and fogs. Overnight, the ground can now become cool enough that when it meets moisture-filled air it chills it to dew point – changing the moisture held in it from invisible water vapour to visible droplets. Air movement in the form of gentle winds keeps these tiny droplets afloat, and a mist or a fog is formed. Both are burned off from the ground upwards: the sun's rays must first penetrate through the fog and warm the ground, which in turn raises the temperature of the air layer above it and that turns the droplets back into invisible water vapour.

December

In the Ancient Meadow

At dawn, the meadow is strewn with cobwebs, which appear as if from nowhere and drape the stubble of plants, glistening with early morning dew or frost. Footprints in the mud suggest the meadow has been busy at night: foxes, deer and badgers roam the land, while hedgehogs sleep.

Sit quietly for a while and you may see a stoat zigzagging across the furthest edges of the meadow, in its ditches or close to a boundary, but never out in the open. They search each area thoroughly, seeking out available food. Stoats mainly eat small mammals, particularly rabbits and water voles. But they also take smaller prey, such as mice and short-tailed field voles, and even earthworms when food is scarce. They kill all but the largest prey with a single bite to the back of the neck, and are sometimes seen dragging their prey under cover. Stoats are known to take over the dens of other animals, including former prey, such as rabbits. In winter they line their stolen dens with rodent fur – often the fur of their prey.

Stoats are masters of camouflage and can turn completely white in winter, to blend in with snow. This rarely happens in mild regions but is common in the north of England and Scotland, where temperatures are lower and chances of significant snowfall are higher. (In Ireland and the Isle of Man, the stoat is a separate subspecies, and does not turn white.) The transformation to 'ermine' (white stoat) is gradual and is triggered by day length and temperature change. Initially a few white hairs may appear on the face and then gradually cover the rest of the body. Some stoats turn completely white, except for the black tip of the tail, while others retain some brown hairs on the face or other parts of the body. The process can take anything from a few weeks to a couple of months.

Kate Bradbury

A Song for December

'Christmas Song' / 'The Trees Are All Bare'

Traditional, arr. Richard Barnard

This beautiful old Christmas tune paints a series of picture postcards of the frozen midwinter countryside, with the meadows at rest, the cattle sending forth their steamy breath, the dairymaid finding flakes of ice on the cream, and the icicles hanging from the eaves. But all is warm and joyful indoors by the fire, where a glass is raised to Christmas, and to the knowledge that spring will soon return.

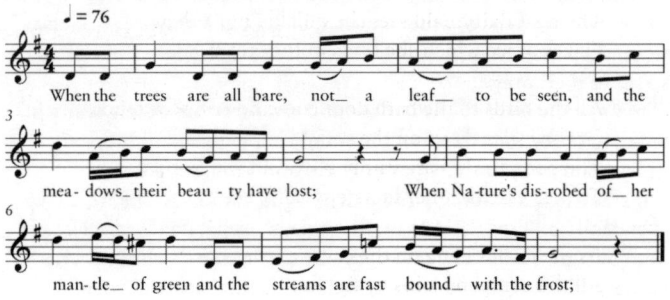

When the trees are all bare, not a leaf to be seen,
And the meadows their beauty have lost;
When Nature's disrobed of her mantle of green
And the streams are fast bound with the frost;

When the labourer stands all a-shivering with cold,
And the northerly winds they do blow;
When innocent flocks run for ease to the fold
With their fleeces all sprinkled with snow,

At the yard where the cattle are foddered with straw
They send forth their breath like a steam.
The neat dairymaid sees she quickly must thaw
Flakes of ice which she finds in the cream.

All the birds to the barn door come hov'ring for food
Or they silently sit on the spray.
The poor, timid hare vainly seeks out the woods,
To take care that her footsteps don't betray.

As the icicles hang on the eaves of the cot
All the company joins by the fire.
Heaven grant that this season it may be our lot
That inside, we can safely retire.

Now Christmas is come and our song we have sung,
And the Spring will return, have no fear;
Come hand to me your glass and I'll drink to your health,
And then wish you a happy New Year.

Nature Table

Mark the Winter Solstice

- Make a nature table with pieces of lichen-covered bark, moss, berried holly, ivy, seed heads, pebbles, old man's beard, feathers and whatever else you can find out-of-doors, then place white candles among everything and light them on the day.
- It is wonderful to catch the sunrise on the winter solstice, even if only from your window, so do it if you can – it certainly happens late enough. As you greet the sun, think about how it will make its lowest arc in the sky today, but how soon it will start to rise higher, lengthen our days and bring spring.
- Fill a spray bottle with water, 1 teaspoon of vodka and 25–30 drops of Christmassy essential oils, then shake it up and spritz it around. Try frankincense, sweet orange or Douglas fir.

Garden and Weather Folklore

We now use the term 'halcyon days' to describe beautiful and endless summer days, but the original phrase referred to the dead of winter. *Halcyon* was the ancient Greek name for the kingfisher, and it was thought it calmed the winter seas, where it built a floating nest in which to lay its eggs. The phrase refers to a period of warm, settled weather around midwinter.

Any significant day in the year attracts weather folklore, and there is, of course, none more significant than Christmas Day. There is an old saying: 'The nearer the new moon to Christmas Day, the harder the winter'. However, take heart because at Christmas: 'If the moon is bright and gleaming, next year's harvest will be poor. If the night is dark with no moon to be seen, harvest will be heavy and bountiful.'

Many of the pieces of Christmas weather lore follow a familiar pattern of 'if the weather is now like this, it will soon change to this' – for instance, 'At Christmas meadows green, at Easter covered with frost' or, more ominously, 'A green Christmas, a full churchyard'.

New Year's Eve, which is also St Sylvester's Day, is another significant day and an occasion to which much lore is attached. Winds are generally considered a bad sign:

'High winds on Sylvester's Day
Will blow the New Year luck away.'

However, the direction of the winds will also set the weather for the coming year:

*'If New Year's Eve the wind blows South,
   It betokeneth warmth and growth
If West, much milk and fish in the sea,
   If North, cold and storms there will be
If East, the trees will bear much fruit,
   If North East, then flee it, man and brute.'*

Migration of the Month

Redwing

By December, most travellers have found a place to hunker down and will not be on the move until spring. There are few migrations in midwinter, for the obvious reason that most creatures migrate in autumn specifically to find a place to sit out this dark and chilly bit. However, a blast of icy weather, should one hit, can put some birds on the move again.

Redwings carried out their main migration back in October. Coming from Russia and Scandinavia, they gathered along the Scandinavian coast and then set off as night fell, completing the 800-km journey across the North Sea in one great flight. They stick together, travelling in flocks, sometimes mixing with fieldfares – other winter migrants who behave in a similar way.

The first call for redwings on reaching Britain and Ireland is the orchards and hedgerows, where they feast on leftover fruits. As winter goes on they take to open farmland and dig for worms among the stubble. But when snow and ice hit, they will move again. After a heavy snowfall, city dwellers may open their curtains to see not just a newly soft and white version of their garden, but also a great flock of redwings and fieldfares perched in a nearby tree. The birds spend these cold winter spells in cities because they are warmer than the open countryside and because there are greater opportunities to find food once autumn's bounty has been gobbled up. Give them fruits and berries, a treat of mealworms and some unfrozen water if you want to help them keep going. When the temperature rises again, they will return to the countryside. Come spring, they migrate back across the North Sea to their breeding grounds in Scandinavia and beyond, their brief but crucial sojourn in our gardens long behind them.

The Hedgerow in December

This is the time of the long sleeps, when the hedgerow inhabitants have tucked themselves back underground or into nooks out of harm's way. The hedgerow's greatest contribution to the lives of its inhabitants now is in creating shelter, filtering winds, sloughing off some of the rains and forming sunny little enclaves at its base. On cold days, you would think that nothing lives in it (though you would be grateful to be standing on the leeward side of it). However, on milder days there can be some tentative venturing out in search of sustenance. Seven-spotted ladybirds will rouse themselves from their crannies and creep along branches on the hunt for overwintering aphids, while badgers will go out foraging whenever there is a decent spell. Even hedgehogs will come out of deepest hibernation and move to a new spot, snuffling for grubs along the way.

You have to look hard for signs of life, but hazel catkins are already starting to fatten and elongate: spring is having ideas even in the depths of winter. Old man's beard is now shedding those fluffy seeds, and they are being lifted by winter winds to drift and hopefully fall on bare ground, where they will wait patiently to germinate in warmer times. Likewise spindle has dropped its orange seeds to take their chances, leaving just the pink wings of the casings dangling prettily. Holly berries are shiny and red against the dark foliage, begging to be plucked by birds or by human foragers. Ivy – always keeping its own time and still producing flowers even in these darkest moments – is just starting to turn some of those flowers to black berries, which will be loved by the birds as the hedgerow heads deeper into winter.

Garden Wildlife in December

In winter, the soil can freeze down to a maximum of about 45cm: a depth known as the frost line. Before this happens, earthworms burrow down into the subsoil, rolling into tight balls and covering themselves with a protective layer of mucus, which enables them to survive without moisture. Amphibians also bury themselves in the soil or tuck themselves beneath stones and logs. Some frogs, particularly males, overwinter at the bottom of ponds, breathing though their skin. In freezing conditions, a frog stops breathing and its heart stops beating – it survives thanks to high levels of glucose in its vital organs. It will thaw out and resume life as soon as temperatures increase.

Some invertebrates, such as springtails, can also survive being frozen for a short period of time, and will simply defrost as temperatures increase again. Bacteria, too, can survive being frozen without injury. Some soil microorganisms remain active, although at a much slower pace. And, while many species of soil fungi don't actively survive winter, setting spores instead, mycorrhizal fungi can remain active, surviving within the root tissues of host plants.

Like soil fauna, perennial plants and trees have evolved to survive freezing conditions. Most plants that evolved to grow in colder climates develop root systems below the frost layer. Freezing can cause root cells to rupture, effectively killing the plant, and so they have nifty ways to prevent it. Plant root cells contain higher concentrations of sugars and salts, which lower the freezing point of water inside them, effectively working as an antifreeze. Roots can also release water into the surrounding soil, minimising damage caused by freezing temperatures.

The healthiest soils play the greatest role in insulating soil fauna and plant roots against the cold. Organic matter, such as leaves and other plant material, as well as mulches of materials like leaf mould or compost, holds on to heat below ground. It won't be long before it all warms up again though, ready for a whole new year of life.

Types of Frost

Hoar frost: From 'hoary', meaning 'aged and whitened', in reference to the shaggy and feathery coating that hoar frost leaves. It occurs under calm, cloudless skies, when there is no (or very little) wind, and under 'inversion' conditions: when cold air is trapped under warmer air.

Advection frost: Strong, cold winds prettily rim the edges of objects and plants with tiny spikes of frost, usually pointing in the direction of the wind.

Window frost: Also known poetically as fern frost or ice flowers, this is the frost that creeps across window frames forming swirls, feathers and other patterns. It is caused by the difference between the very cold air on the outside of the glass and the warmer, moderately moist air on the inside. The growth of the patterns responds to imperfections on the glass surface.

Folk Song of the Month

'Cherry Tree Carol'

Traditional, arr. Richard Barnard

This very old song is known to have been sung since at least the 15th century. Mary and Joseph are travelling to Bethlehem when they pass a cherry orchard and Mary asks Joseph to gather some cherries for her. When he refuses – 'Let him gather thee cherries that got thee with child' – Jesus pipes up from the womb and makes sure Mary gets her cherries before a chastened Joseph. There are many variations and this tune is closest to a traditional Cornish version.

O, Joseph was an old man,
And an old man was he,
And Joseph married Mary,
The Queen of Galilee.

So Joseph and Mary
Through a garden did go,
Where cherries a-plenty
On every tree did grow.

O, then bespoke Mary
With words meek and mild,
'O, gather me cherries,
For I am with child.'

And then replied Joseph
with words so unkind,
'Let him gather thee cherries
That got thee with child.'

O, then bespoke our Saviour
In his mother's womb,
'Bow down, good cherry tree
For to give my mother some.'

The uppermost sprig
It bowed down to Mary's knee,
'Thus you may see, Joseph,
These cherries are for me.'

EDIBLE CLAMS

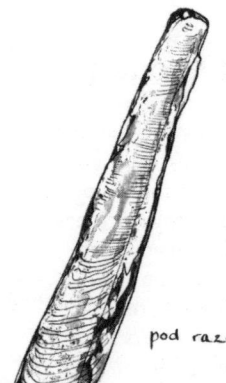
pod razor

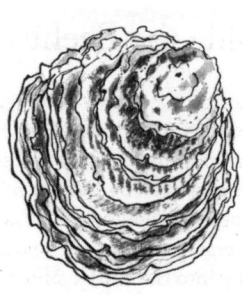
european flat oyster

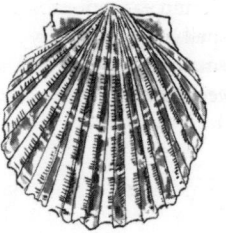
queen scallop

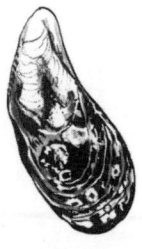
blue mussel

sea cockle

Inside the Beehive in December

As the shortest day arrives, activity inside the beehive comes almost to a complete halt. Supplies must be eked out and that means minimal activity (except, perhaps, for hymn singing at midnight on Christmas Eve). The colony comes together into the 'winter cluster', a ball-shaped grouping across several of the hives. The outer bees line up side by side, facing into the cluster, and so creating a thermal layer. Normally this will be one bee thick, but as temperatures drop there can be several layers of insulating bees. Within the cluster the temperature can be mild enough for the bees to move around a little and eat some honey. The bees take it in turns to have a spell inside. In really cold weather, the cluster will contract, maintaining heat in a small area and keeping the bees alive until milder days come.

Look Out For

Short-Eared and Tawny Owls

Short-eared owls are among the few owls to regularly hunt in broad daylight. In winter they move to wetlands and coastal marshes, so if you find yourself out on a winter walk in such a spot, look out for them gliding silently in search of prey. You are less likely to spot a tawny owl, but they are at their noisiest in December, particularly at dusk, making their distinctive call and response 'two-wit' 'two-woo' as they seek a mate.

Flower of the Month

Christmas Rose

Latin name: *Helleborus niger* (*Helleborus*, from the Middle
English *ellebore* and/or the Greek *helleboros* – a name
given to plants that are both poisonous and medicinal;
niger, Latin for 'black', perhaps referring to the roots).
Common names: hellebore.

Legend says that the Christmas rose sprouted when the tears of a young girl who had no gift to give the baby Jesus fell on the snow. *Helleborus niger* is certainly as pretty as a snowy Christmas card, with its pure white, simple flowers just begging for a robin to perch nearby – but, in fact, the species does not reliably flower at Christmas and can kick in a little later. Disappointing. However, breeding efforts have been concentrated on bringing that flowering season forward, so if you go to the garden centre this month and buy a hellebore while it is in flower, you should have one that can be decked with outdoor fairy lights every year.

Hellebores do well in the ground, but their downward-facing blooms can get a little lost. They work better in pots that can be lifted up onto tables, or placed either side of the front door for December.